PENGUIN BOOKS

THE BASKETBALL DIARIES

Poet, musician, and diarist Jim Carroll was born and grew up in New York City. Talented at both basketball and writing, he attended Trinity High School in Manhattan on a scholarship and was an All-City basketball star, a period in his life vividly described in *The Basketball Diaries*. Carroll's first collection of poetry, *Living at the Movies*, was published in 1973 when he was twenty-two. His other books include a novel, *The Petting Zoo*; a second memoir, *Forced Entries: The Downtown Diaries 1971–1973*, and the poetry collections *The Book of Nods*, *Fear of Dreaming*, and *Void of Course*. As a leader of the Jim Carroll Band, he released three albums for Atlantic records as well as several spoken word recordings. Jim Carroll died in New York City on September 11, 2009.

THE
BASKETBALL
DIARIES

JIM CARROLL

PENGUIN BOOKS

PENGUIN BOOKS
Published by the Penguin Group
Penguin Group (USA) Inc., 375 Hudson Street, New York, New York 10014, U.S.A.
Penguin Group (Canada), 90 Eglinton Avenue East, Suite 700, Toronto, Ontario,
Canada M4P 2Y3 (a division of Pearson Penguin Canada Inc.)
Penguin Books Ltd, 80 Strand, London WC2R 0RL, England
Penguin Ireland, 25 St Stephen's Green, Dublin 2, Ireland
(a division of Penguin Books Ltd)
Penguin Group (Australia), 250 Camberwell Road, Camberwell, Victoria 3124, Australia
(a division of Pearson Australia Group Pty Ltd)
Penguin Books India Pvt Ltd, 11 Community Centre, Panchsheel Park,
New Delhi – 110 017, India
Penguin Group (NZ), 67 Apollo Drive, Rosedale, North Shore 0632,
New Zealand (a division of Pearson New Zealand Ltd)
Penguin Books (South Africa) (Pty) Ltd, 24 Sturdee Avenue, Rosebank,
Johannesburg 2196, South Africa

Penguin Books Ltd, Registered Offices: 80 Strand, London WC2R 0RL, England

First published in the United States of America by Tombouctou Books 1978
Published in Penguin Books 1987

39 40

Copyright © Jim Carroll, 1963, 1964, 1965, 1966, 1967, 1968, 1969, 1970, 1971,
1972, 1973, 1974, 1975, 1976, 1977, 1978
All rights reserved

Some portions of *The Basketball Diaries* have appeared in the following magazines:
*The World, Adventures in Poetry, Little Caesar, The Ant's Forefoot, The Paris Review,
Big Sky, Spectrum,* and *Culture Hero,* and in the following anthologies: *The World
Anthology* (Bobbs-Merrill), *Another World* (Bobbs-Merrill),
and on the records *Dial-A-Poem* and *Disconnected.*

LIBRARY OF CONGRESS CATALOGING IN PUBLICATION DATA
Carroll, Jim.
The basketball diaries.
I. Title.
PS3553.A7644B35   1987   813'.54   87-25496
ISBN 978-0-14-010018-1 (pbk.)

Printed in the United States of America
Set in Baskerville

Special thanks to
Anne Waldman, Ted Berrigan,
Patti Smith and Bill Berkson

IN MEMORY OF PHIL OCHS

THE BASKETBALL DIARIES

FALL 1963

FALL 63

Today was my first Biddy League game and my first day in any organized basketball league. I'm enthused about life due to this exciting event. The Biddy League is a league for anyone 12 yrs. old or under. I'm actually 13 but my coach Lefty gave me a fake birth certificate. Lefty is a great guy; he picks us up for games in his station wagon and always buys us tons of food. I'm too young to understand about homosexuals but I think Lefty is one. Although he's a great ballplayer and a strong guy, he likes to do funny things to you like put his hand between your legs and pick you up. When he did this I got keenly suspicious. I guess I better not tell my mother about it. I don't want to describe the first game; I played bad and we lost anyway. I was nervous, I took my girl-friend Joan to the game which was at 153rd St., a Negro church called Minisink. Our team is from Madison Sq. Boys Club on E. 29th St. The starting team consists of two Italians, two spades and me.

When the game was over and we were waiting on the subway platform at 155th, Tony Milliano started a fight with Kevin Dolon. Tony is a huge monster who loves to fight; Kevin is a wise ass little prick. Some guys tried to break it up but Tony wouldn't let them and kept on yelling, "I want blood!" It was scary but interesting; I don't like to fight but I love watching others fight. Kevin asked me to jump Milliano from behind but he was too big for me to get involved. Who wanted to help that little fucker anyway? He's forever getting me in trouble down at St. Agnes grade school, where we go. Just today he snitched to Sister Mary Grace about me spitting on the first graders from the lunch room window.

FALL 63

It was the warmest October day that I ever saw today, so we skipped practice (Tony and Yogi and I) and decided to take a little ride down to the ferry and over to Staten Island. After polishing off a hero at LUCY'S we hopped on the back fender of the Second Ave. bus and rode down to the ferry basin. Once I fell off a bus like that on a sharp turn and almost got my balls crushed under the back wheel, but this ride was smooth enough and we got off and deposited our nickels in the turnstiles and were off. Just as the boat is pulling out of the dock, Tony takes out a bottle of CARBONA cleaning fluid and a few rags and suggests that we do a little sniffing to get high. I was up for this idea because Carbona is one of the finest cheap highs you can get, even stronger than model glue. We slipped up to the top deck of the ship and wet our rags and raised them to our faces. After four deep whiffs we were sailing someplace else, bells ringing through my ears and little lights flashing through my eyes. I pictured myself paddling across a river with black water, only the canoe was going backwards instead of forwards, with clouds that were faces laughing spooky fun-house laughs which wouldn't stop echoing. More sniffs and more freaky visions, the ringing bell sound always getting louder the more I breathe the stuff into my lungs. I kept it up for about ten minutes, but by then I was getting too dizzy to handle it and I had to fling down the rag and make it to the side rail, sick as possible. I began puking wildly. My eyes felt like bowling balls and they were watering like mad. Tony and Yogi had done themselves in too and they ran over to join in the ceremony. Then we recovered enough to hear shouts from the bottom deck and wiping off our eyes we realized that we had zeroed in over the head of some dude. More unfortunate was the fact that the guy was fantastically huge and looked horribly pissed. We wasted no time in making it to the nearest hiding spot, knowing the guy would be up after us any second. We got to the other side of the boat and did a quick Steve McQueen act, over the rail and down to the lowest deck. Then we ducked into the bathroom and into the last toilet stall, locking the door and sweating our balls off. We hung on in there, reading the little pencilled-in obscenities until the boat docked. After about ten minutes we sent Yogi out to see if the coast was clear. He came back and signalled us out and we ran our asses off the boat, through the terminal onto the nearest bus. We came to a nice park somewhere in the middle of the island and played ball with the local weaklings all day, taking on everyone, even guys as old as sixteen or so. It was almost dark when we caught our ferry back to the city again, keeping a sharp lookout for our friend and vowing we'd never sniff that stuff on any ferry again.

FALL 63

They finally took away old Mrs. McNulty today. She was the incredibly nutty lady who lived right across the alley from our window in the building. She had a very scary habit of going to her sink every night in her bra and panties and offering Mass over it as if it were her altar. She knew the Mass inside out, but she would interject incredible obscenities whenever the Virgin Mary's name came up, or Christ's name too, for that matter. She had all the standard equipment for the Mass, a gold chalice and all the rest, but at the part that appeared to be what the Catholics considered the consecration, she would shove the thing between her legs and yell, "Suck me, eat my puss, God." Things like that. The stuff she laid down about Mary was always the worst, and I would watch everything quite clearly and really shudder; not that I was ever really religious (not since I was eight actually, when one day I went into a church for the first time and tried to make friends with God by asking him to come home with me so we could watch the World Series together) but because I couldn't understand at all what the fuck could ever possess someone to do something as fruity as that. Man, she really let fly some nights, yelling so that everyone in the building could hear her. When I told some friends about her, a lot of them wanted to come over to see, thinking the scene was really sexy or something. But she was an old lady, sixty-five at least, so the sight of her dressed like that and freaking the way she did was too disgusting, I always had to turn away. I guess someone complained once too often lately and I saw her being tucked into an ambulance, very calm about it, while I was coming back from school today.

FALL 63

All us little crooks down here on the lower east side got one specialty in common: snatching hand bags off ladies. It started first with the bad-off junkies but now it's worked down to us, The Diaper Bandits (as the paper called us in a story in last night's issue). The dumbest move is to snatch on your own streets. People know all the other people around this yack-yack neighborhood. So we go uptown in the east 60s and posh spots like that in little packs and spread out in the dark and work in teams or, maybe after awhile, alone. One guy walks up to the lady to ask the way to the subway and if you're lucky she points and holds her arm out straight with the bag on her wrist and the other guy swipes it and you're both off. If that don't work you give yourself five seconds tugging time (the most since by then she's calling in the troops) then scratch her up as a loss and tear ass; only the real strung-out junkies go in for rapping them out if they put up a fight, but I'm scared enough without doing a regular mug job. This is my diary for tonight 'cause it was my best day. This lady we pulled the directions-bit on had $123 and change, and that is big time. Then she had a book of traveler's checks that ain't no good for us but that Yogi's big brother bought for five. He says they're good as cash. Most people think this is pulled only on old ladies but this woman tonight was something to jerk off to, as a bonus. Probably a fruit too, 'cause she had all these pictures of nude ladies in the bag; not the dirty mag. ones either. These didn't just show the tits but the cunts too. They were Polaroid snapshots someone took themselves. One was two ladies frenching each other and another was a whole series with girls giving blow-jobs to guys. This one scene had seven people in it doing shit I never heard of. But the topper was one of a fat ugly bitch getting screwed on a table by, I swear, a donkey . . . that was the biggest hit ever at the Boys' Club. Herb's big brother says he used to see that in some nightclub in Mexico when he was in the Navy. We, Carson my partner and I, were selling these pictures for three bucks each and got rid of all ten, except this one of some sexy lady on a bed throwing this big hairy spread. She had a smile on her face that seemed to say, "Everything is perfectly OK." That one turned me on too much. So we split the profits and went home—the diaper bandits strike again.

FALL 63

Lefty drove us up to the Bronx this afternoon to play some Catholic school in a Biddy exhibition game. A few of the guys were sick, so many, in fact, that we only had five men to start the game and when Carson fouled out in the last period we had to finish out with only four men on the court. No matter, it was the lamest bunch of saps ever put on a court, this other team, and we wiped them out by at least forty points. Lefty sure can pick them. So after the swamp we realized there was another bonus to be had besides winning . . . Carson had snuck into the other team's lockers after he got the boot and wiped out their valuables. We forced him into splitting up the take and we slipped our clothes on over our uniforms, no showers, of course, and made a fast split out.

When we reached Fordham Rd. down the block, we got Lefty to pull his car into the hamburger joint's lot and put the bite on him for some burgers. Everyone kept their mouths tight about looting the other team 'cause there are two things Lefty forbids: using the word

"Motherfucker" and stealing from another team so long as they're white. Inside the place he made it an order that we get only one burger each but we all said fuck it to that 'cause the burgers were those twelve cent skimpy jobs and you've got to get at least eight or more to get filled at all, and that's just what we did. This distressed Lefty no end because the bill came to something like nine bucks and all he had was a fiver. It caused a big scene and embarrassed Lefty, who had to leave his watch with the manager until he got the bread to him. Lefty got the last laugh on us though because he hopped into his station wagon in a steam and refused to drive us back to the lower east side. This upset us very much seeing that the bunch of guys we had just robbed were heading toward us in the parking lot with assorted pipes etc. ready to kick our Biddy asses. "Face the music, Pricks," chimed Lefty as he tooled out leaving rubber, leaving us too, running our behinds down Fordham Rd. where we luckily mobbed into a cab and pulled out toward the nearest downtown subway with a crowd of angry Catholic ballplayers and their friends, led by a tough looking Italian priest, his robe flowing, behind us.

FALL 63

A whole bunch of us were hitching rides on the back of the bus down Third Ave. tonight toward 10th St. where we walked over to our rival game at the Tompkins Sq. Boys' Club. There's four of us each on the back of two back-to-back buses & it's cool until 14th St. where the cops spot us and we scatter across the street. They don't bother to chase us so we bop on when out of the pink Herbie points across the street where all the whores hang out and shouts to Pedro that his mother is over there with them all and everyone starts to goof on the sap. But the blow is that Herbie wasn't cracking on him for a goof and Pedro's mom is really over there hustling, leaning with one foot up on the building and the whole bit. Then Tony leans over to me and mumbles, "Dig that, I heard my big sister say one night to my old lady when I was on the sneak that Pedro's pop dealt junk down the bar and both of them was on the H; now dig this, he got the old lady out hustling." When everyone saw it was really his old lady they cooled the goofing but Pedro already was out of sight. He didn't show up for the game either but after we beat the suckers down there by ten points and were going home, we walked by Pedro who was on his stoop on 27th St. He ran in crying I think. It must be a bitch having a family like that, damn. Herbie has no feelings about it though and he kept yelling up to Pedro's window: "Why did the little shoe cry? 'Cause his father was a loafer & his mother was a sneaker!"

FALL 63

This afternoon Pedro's big brother grabbed Herbie on the way home from school and beat the shit out of him 'cause of what Herbie was yelling about Pedro's mom and pop last night.

FALL 63

There was a giant fire on Second Ave. tonight that did in three buildings on the corner of 25th St. The flames were real cloud-singeing motherfuckers, twice as high as the buildings themselves. I never saw a fire like it. A whole gang of us laughed our nuts off because the pizza-man was out on the street, I swear, right down on his knees begging the firemen not to break in the new all-glass front he had just built for the place a month ago. The dope was crying; the place was totally up in smoke and he thinks some miracle's gonna bring it back or some shit. Good for the big bastard, he never gives credit and he won't even let you use the bathroom in the joint. Now the big tough guy is down on his knees in the street. Musta taken five hours to put this one out. The flames at one point were higher than my bedroom window.

By the way: I heard that Herbie's big brother and his boys beat the living shit out of Pedro's big brother because of the way Pedro's big brother beat up Herbie yesterday. That thing is gonna blow up to a gang war soon.

FALL 63

It's a cold Saturday and the Boys' Club is closed for repairs so I figure I'll take a trip up to the tip of Manhattan where my cousin lives and give him a little visit. Actually I hate that scene 'cause the place is filled with all these Irish Catholic old biddies who gave me a lot of stares one time when I brought a bunch of black guys up there to play ball in the park against my cousin's friends, a bunch of black haters too, who are into this real heavy beer drinking thing. But then again a lot of them are good people once you dig them and besides I better get used to it because I've got to move up there with my family soon and finish the second half of the year at the school all these cats attend.

So I throw a can of pink lemonade into a pitcher and drink the whole quart for breakfast, then walk over to the west side to catch the "A" train uptown. It's such a long fucking ride up there, all the way to the last stop on the line at 207th St. It's like I was taking a trip to Albany and I'm glad I brought along this sports mag. to break the boredom. So I'm reading this piece on how Bill Russell is gonna eat up "Wilt the Stilt" and all is well until I reach 125th and onto the train stumbles this old Irish drunk and he sits right next to me, smelling like a brewery and laying this gibberish sob drama on me; it never fails. Like I hate these old peckers, but I think they search through trains looking for me, you know, because in a half-filled car they'll always pass up anyone else and come right over to me either cursing insane, bumming coin or worst of all the old sob routine. The trouble with me is I never have the nerve to tell them to fuck off, or go find another seat myself, so what happens is that about two stops later I'm really involved with the dumb story the dude is laying on me (though I can't understand half of what he's saying) and I even start rapping back like "Yeah, I know just what you mean, the same thing happened to a man I knew and he became a drunk from it and blah, blah, etc."

You know, taking the dude really serious as if he were making sense. This particular fruit today took the cake.

He kept leaning all over me with his drooling mug telling me how he killed his wife by accident by dropping a big mirror on her head as they were putting it up together or some shit like that and every ten seconds sticking a bottle of "Twister" in my face asking me to take a drink. So anyway as usual the transit cop comes along at 181st St. and kicks the guy off and the guy gives me this pathetic sad wave good-bye as the train was pulling out like he was thinking, "Who's gonna listen to me now?" and I felt blank and sad like always after that happens.

FALL 63

We didn't have any school today because tomorrow is Halloween. I went to hang out with the other guys at the Boys' Club over on 29th and met Herbie and the bunch upstairs playing pool. I figured it would be the perfect goof to hang out with these cats tonight so we went up to the gym and around the stoops and rounded-up a few more jack-offs, smeared shoe polish on our faces and ripped the sleeves on our shirts a bit for a bummed out costume effect. Buddy, one of the few spades to hang out with Herbie and his boys, didn't need any polish of course and not much ripping either, in fact, 'cause he was sort of bummy in his effect any day, Halloween or not. Then we got some extra long socks from one of the guys' old man who had varicose veins, filled them up with flour and began to attack the girls in their dark school dresses going to the dance over at the church, the flour streaking giant white marks across their backs. They were quite a joke running down the block threatening to tell the nuns on us and all. Man, who gave the slightest fuck what the goddamn nuns thought anyway . . . I wasn't in the Catholic school any more so those fucking penguins were not going to screw my ass one bit longer.

For our next wise-ass goof we go upstairs in the nearest building and place a paper bag, filled with dog shit, in front of the top apartment door, set the bag on fire and tear ass down to the lower floor and listen while some old bugger stomps on the bag to put out the fire. I could almost hear the expression on the creep's face, wiping his slippers off over the john with tissue paper.

Down on 24th we found a bunch of little kiddies trick-or-treating. Buddy the spade broke an egg over the head of one little blonde girl dressed up as an angel. She ran off crying, yolk on the wings. Is nothing sacred to wise asses? Not tonight. Especially after Herbie's big brother scored us some wine and we all got wrecked and got the idea to fill our socks up with gravel instead of flour and beat ass off the creeps over in the new projects, breaking windows, dodging cops across rooftops, all kinds of crazy shit until three in the morning. I finally snuck in with everyone else sound in bed, but it doesn't matter because my old man is sure to beat my ass tomorrow because I got real sick from that red wine and puked all over the new rug in the hallway.

FALL 63

We played tonight in some big time 13-year-old and younger tournament way far up in the Bronx, a ritzy neighborhood called Riverdale . . . giant stone private houses . . . lots of ivy and swimming pools, that whole bit. It seemed like a trip to Utica from down here at the Boys' Club on E. 29th, but Lefty drives like a bitch so it wasn't too bad. Carson managed to get car sick again and he couldn't hold it back so he had to puke into one of Lefty's leather work gloves that we found under a spare tire in the back of the wagon. No one told Lefty about that though, so cheers to him next time some work pops up that needs gloves. We arrived at the gym of Riverdale High and the place was pretty fucking fancy, you bet your ass. Plenty of light from nice high ceilings and lots of lame basketball fans in the stands. We go to the locker rooms right away since we're half an hour late already. Our team is good at getting dressed quick because we're the type of team that wears their uniforms all day. Game or no game, we just don't dig carrying around those little fag bags with our stuff in them, we just whip off our shirt and pants and we're out on the court in a minute. After the game, it was the same thing, no showers, of course, just up with our pants and on with our shirts and out the door.

So we go onto the court and here are these guys we're playing all duded up in blue and gold uniforms with little stars all over them, and going through these perfect warm-up drills. We were pretty raggy next to those guys but we went over o.k. with the crowd because we're these tough raggamuffins from the lower east side, all poor and shaggy, and all these nice parents who have a few cars and smoke pipes and shit, well, they were gonna cheer the underdogs from the ghetto right along, whip-pie, that was so nice of them. So we took a few warm-up shots and went over and sat down and Lefty told us

to use the press against them from the start. By the end
of the first four minutes we were ahead by 23 points
and the pretty boys from Lake Peekskill, or wherever
the fuck they were from, didn't know what to do. They
called a timeout. We stopped the press out of sheer pity
and the rest of the half wasn't as exciting. They seemed
to all have lead in their asses and never heard of the
word "drive," so we constantly drove in for easy show-
off layups or feeds to our big men. We fast broke so
much Lefty told us to cool it before the guys that ran
the thing started checking birth certificates and finding
out that half our guys were ringers. One of our forwards,
this tall spade with a baby face, must have been playing
in these 13 and under farces for the past ten years, no
shit. Score 53–20, at the half.

The locker room during the half was one of the most
uncool scenes during the season. Three of our guys got
caught by Lefty sniffing glue in the toilet stalls. I was
lucky to flush down mine in time so old coachie thought
I was in there legit. Lefty would take a lot of shit but he
didn't dig any glue sniffing, so those suckers had to sit
out the second half. Another thing that strangely enough
really pisses off Lefty is anyone using that popular little
expression "motherfucker," as if he, who has no hesi-
tations about grabbing guys' balls and cocks in the middle of the team prayer in the huddle before the game,
was some great moralist or something. Anyway, with the
other starters out, I get to score all the points and wind
up with 42, which felt good because I haven't really
been scoring that many lately. I can also see little Most
Valuable Player trophies in my head if this keeps up.
We won by an awful lot. After the game they gave us
free sodas and shit and all the local people stood in the

lobby as we left and patted us on the back and said, "Nice game, son," and all, the whole scene strictly out of "Leave It To Beaver," all the old men Fred MacMurray types in tweed suits and the women, a pack of poodle walkers, standing around with a lot of make-up and sort of thinking how cute we were. They had these teased up bleached hair-dos that reminded me exactly of the higher priced 14th St. whores. I wanted to ask one if she wanted to suck it off but we just hopped into the car for that bitch trip downtown. It's a Friday night and we all wanted to go to the East River Park and get drunk, do reefer and sniff glue. And that's exactly what we did.

FALL 63

Today we moved our last piece of furniture into our apartment in my new neighborhood at the upper tip of Manhattan. I've been up here before and got a pretty good image of the general bullshit of the local population. Fuck, they take the lamest cake in town. Hallways in my new building and each park bench filled with chattering old Irish ladies either gossiping or saying the rosary, or men long time here or younger ones right off the boat huddling in floppy overcoats in front of drug stores discussing their operations, ball scores, or the Commie threat. Guys my age strictly All-American, though most of the various crowds do the beer-drinking scene on weekends. My cousin Kevin did introduce me to a few weed-heads up here once, and today I ran into them and goofed with some ball playing. Most likely they'll be my scene. Nice basketball courts around here, at least.

Of course, the worst bullshit about this move is having to go back to a fucking Catholic school just in the middle of a goof year in a Public joint. That scene is simple, Catholic schools are sheer shit, madmen in fucking collars who in their pious minds can never be wrong, running around with their rubber straps beating asses red for the least little goofing, and pushing into a bunch of stiff noodle-sized brains that "Who made us? . . . ," "God made us . . . ," horse drip. The old biddy penguins they call nuns are even worse. I'm cracking back the first cat who tries that "bend over" shit, hoping they give me the boot quick. I've already got a scholarship set for that plush Private School next year, so I'm going to breeze easy for the rest of this grammar school bit. I'm meeting Kevin in the morning and we're supposed to get drunk, it'll be cool 'cause then I can pull the "sleeping over at his house" bit and not get snagged by Moms. I'll tell her the smell of paint gets me sick 'cause they're painting tomorrow; that ought to work.

FALL 63

My cousin's parents are away for the weekend so Chris, Willie, me and my cousin went up there right after school and raided the liquor cabinet. My cousin lives in the ritzy part of the neighborhood up on Park Terrace and they've got this swank penthouse with a real little bar and the whole shit. It's an extra lucky scene because it's a freezing your ass off day out and we couldn't hang out in the park and all so we plan to make a weekend of it up there, keeping it cool so not many jack-offs come roaring in and mess the place. Last time his parents went off, two lamps got busted and Fat Eddie puked all over the new sofa. Fat Eddie will definitely not be up here again . . . you can still smell the puke on that fucking sofa to this day. So we bought a batch of orange juice for screwdrivers and made ourselves comfy sitting on the little bar stools feeling cool.

In about two hours things went down like this: I was a little tipsy, but not bad, because I always just keep puking if I really get smashed and that is no fun. Chris cannot hold liquor for his asshole's sake but he's a well known "spiller" so he was mostly putting on a drunk act. A "spiller" is the guy who wants to say he had as much as everyone else but knows he'd be floored if he did, so he's always sneaking over to the window or making fifty trips to the john and spilling half or more of his drink away and then asking for another. I watched him in the park one night when he claimed he drank a case of beer but everytime I saw him open a can he'd take one sip and toss it down the hill, everyone else could tell too cause his cans always made a "thud" while everyone else's made a tinny sound. My cousin had to make sure he was sober enough to not start calling up every minor in the neighborhood and have the place in bits. He was just sort of light and giddy like me, about the stage when you start bullshitting about all the girls you fucked and pooling info on how much the chicks in the crowd go . . . Anyway we were in walking shape. Then there was Willie who said before that he was really gonna lay it on and, fuck, he sure did. He was blind drunk, couldn't even make it to the john by himself, and had to have one of us holding him while he pissed. Then he fell and smashed his head open on the tub. He started to yell and scream zonked nonsense and busted a tiny statue of some saint with a fucking bird on its head. Cousin Kevin went shit-house over that and decided we ought to take the jerk out and sober him up. The prick ruined our whole scene, it was freezing out and by now snowing fairly hard. Kevin and I each took an arm and started to walk him down the street to the park and Chris, who quit his drunk act by now, was scraping the thin layer of snow off cars and rubbing it in his mug but nothing helped. He was quiet now 'cause he seemed like he was konking out but near the park entrance we met up with Deborah Duckster, this chick in our neighborhood who's a model with one of those portfolios they carry and all, on her way home. Willie was lunging for her and trying to grab her and he broke away from us and just as he was a foot or two away from us she poked him a direct hit in the nuts and shuffled off cursing. Willie was on the pave-ment in agony and we put more snow in his face but the prick konked out on us right there and we had to drag his dead weight into the park. Near the ball field we're slapping him around and shaking him and shit but no bet. We were worried he might have to get his stomach pumped like another dude in our class last week. Then we were snagged good . . . A cop saw us and came chugging over. "Holy shit" was my simple reaction. He gets over to the flaked out body and bends over to check his eyes and looks up with hideous stare and grinds out in tough cop voice, "You guys been sniffing glue?" Now this surprised me, because it would be a very common question down in my old neighborhood in the East 20s but cops up here never think any kid around this Irish hole in upper, upper Manhattan uses drugs, even glue; usually a blue boy around here takes for granted the sap is just a plain cold drunk. Could be this fuzz got transferred from some drug neighborhood recently. Anyway we all chimed in quick "no"s to him and he believed us there 'cause of the shock on our mugs of him even suggesting glue and the quickness of our answers. Meanwhile I'm digging away for a legit excuse like having gotten hit by a baseball, no, no chance on that one, it's early February for Christ's sake. Then out of the blue old master mind Chris spurts out in one shaky gulp, "Well, you see officer, like he was sleigh riding and lost control and hit his head on a lamp post and passed out." That was a beauty, real real genius, the dumb fuck: first of all we ain't got a sled, second there ain't even a fucking hill in sight, third, and not least, it had been snowing the first snow of the entire winter for about twenty goddamn minutes, like there wasn't enough snow on the entire ball field to make two snow balls and here is this jerk ass talking about a sleigh accident . . . Jesus Christ! The cop was almost laughing himself and looked at Chris and just mumbled and shook his head. The man told us in a friendly voice that was no fake that we just better tell what happened 'cause Willie might be fucked up worse than we thought. We looked at each other, nodded in agreement, and I said what the fuck and told him he was just smashed on booze and nothing more. So the man took some snow and rubbed Willie's mug one more time and he got no better results than us. Then he slapped him a bit and nothing, not a fucking batted eyelash, man, he was like a frozen pack of string beans or something. The cop gave up and called an ambulance on the cop phone in the park house. Nothing else to do, I figured, but Willie has a strict mother and he was sure to get fucked over bad. The cats in the white suits got there in a snap and off went the poor cat to get the pump job, and back we went to a warm penthouse and turned on the t.v. just in time for "Superman."

WINTER 1964

WINTER 64

Once a month as an eighth grader in this screwy Catholic school we got to march over to church after school's out to go to confession. I was baptized a Catholic and all, but my moms and pops never go to church except maybe Christmas to hear the shit choir croak out them goodies, and in fact they never made us go either. So I never made first communion or got confirmed or whatever it is and least of all been to confession. Besides, we usually get out early on Friday. Now they throw this shit at me and a friend tells me you've got to wait until everyone is finished, and it might take an hour maybe if there are only a few priests handy to dish whatever they do out. I tried to beg off, telling the Brother that I never did any of this stuff before, but he gave me a very freaky look and told me to get in line. So we're in the giant church and he sticks me on line and I say, "But, I never, I swear . . ." No good, the dumb bastard don't even listen and at that moment let me tell you I hated that fucking school and that whole religion worse than anything before with their tiny dark boxes you enter like they were phone booths to God. They should gun off the whole bunch, they're fucking up minds they do not own. I was gonna just split and run, but all the while I was also curious to dig what went on through these finely carved doors in and out of which each cat was going. I really wanted to find out the story. When my turn comes I'm nervous and the Brother is still on me with the evil-eye. Inside you've got to kneel; I caught on and I could hear the priest mumbling back and forth to the guy on the other side but I couldn't hear in. He was taking a long time with the dude, so that cat must have been fucking off quite a bit. Then, pow, he slides open a little door and says my turn but he can't see me or me him . . . just listen. "What the fuck now?" I ask myself, and he must have thought I was nervous so he started me off and then I froze up totally. He asked me what was up (not in those words, dig) and I said, "Priest, I ain't never done this before because like I'm not really Catholic and the Brother out there made me come in but I told him I . . . well, shit" (I really said shit too and then said excuse me and all), "I don't know what to say." The man knew I was shitting in my pants and told me it wasn't my fault and just step out and don't worry about a thing. He was an o.k. mug. Then as I got out I jumped back 'cause the door in the middle opened and the priest burst out in a purple-faced nut-attack and started to lay some heavy shit on the Brother that sent me in there in the first place, calling him a fool and a disgrace to his fellow robe-wearers. The whole class was goofing on the prick, and the friends I'd made lately by playing punchball at lunch were looking at me and shaking their heads and goofing. None of these guys dug the lame and they loved the scene almost as much as me, and I think quick that if the brother gives me any shit about it, I'm going right back to that priest, and he knows it too. Meanwhile we all filed out and I made it down to the club, only for our team to get its ass wiped by the first place team. But I hit for 27 and along with the other scene my day was cool.

WINTER 64

Today is our last Biddy League game of the year, but before it all the members of the Boys' Club have to meet in front of the place to have some kind of memorial service for little Teddy Rayhill. He's a member of the club that fell off the roof the other day while he was sniffing glue. The priest was making a speech about Teddy and tried to pawn off some story about him fixing a TV antenna when he fell off but no one swallowed that shit. In the middle of the service Herbie Hemslie and his gang started flinging bricks down from the roof across the street. Everybody had to clear out into the club while the cops chased after Herbie and friends. After it was safe to go out again, everybody filed past Teddy's closed casket and if you wanted to you said a prayer. If you didn't want to I guess you just stood and felt shitty about everything.

WINTER 64

This Catholic school bullcrap takes the lemon right into your eye. Dig it, we get these weekly report cards based on homework and tiny tests sprung here and there and this week I got a god damm 99 on the thing and in the "effort" column the smart ass Brother gave me a "D," for what reason I can't figure. So the principal comes around and hands them out on Friday and for the effort bullshit he tells me to take a stand over on the side with a bunch of other chumps, mostly guys who failed the whole bit and I get three raps across the hand with this

thick rubber strap, it fucking hurt too, and this with a
99 grade, what these mothers expect is beyond me. All
the back-collared asses got them rubber straps, except
Bro. Wally Whale, so called, who is my geography teach
and he uses a thin little wooden stick across the ass that
stings all day. I want to get back in public school so bad,
and I know I should just belt back the next prick who
hits me, but something holds me back. I guess deep
down I think they have the right to boss me around.
I've got to break loose.

WINTER 64

Today's school day should be up for "Ripley's Believe
It Or Not." Right during morning prayers Billy "Dong"
Burlap threw a beauty of an epileptic fit, tossing himself
over his desk in the middle of an "Our Father" and
drooling and chomping and spinning down the aisle.
Somebody ran for Brother Kenneth, the only good dude
in the joint, because he's used to handling Dong's frequent fits from last year and because our Brother, a
snoot intellectual but all freeze in a clutch, didn't know
what the hell to do. A few more maniac moves and Dong
got cooled. Bro. Kenny's hand was bloody from teeth
bites as he tried to get ahold of Billy's tongue so he
wouldn't choke on it. His whole hand was scarred from
handling fits over the years. Then Billy got taken down
to the nurse to lay down and wait for his moms. Some
"nurse." You could walk in with an eight-inch gash on
your mug and she'd give you a Band-Aid and aspirin.

In fact, come in with anything and all you get is an aspirin. Well, that was Dong's performance. Then, maybe an hour later, Donny Levy, also a regular fit flinger but not as bad as Dong, falls into one of his vegetable states. He rarely gets the going-ape type fit, but very often he suddenly flies right off into another galaxy. He is still, except for a steady shake and has no idea what or where he is and starts picking his nose and doing things in slow motion with a weird stare like those kids in the flick, "Village of the Damned." I handled him through one when he was up at my house so I went and talked to him in a gentle tone but really he can't tell I'm there. Sometimes he goes into a "Dong" type fit if he ain't getting comforted but lucky this time he cooled out of it after a while, though he's still in a daze, and it's to the nurse with him so his moms can pick him up too. After lunch, this gigantic Spanish dude, Carlo Puzo, who is new in school like me, falls flat on his mug with a surprise faint and with bloody face starts rolling and kicking and there's eight of us trying to pin him down but he's got the strength of a horse. So we finally take care of him and the teach looks up and waves his hand up and says flatly, "Anyone else?" I'm home now checking the almanac to see if there's any record on fits tossed in one class of thirty people in one half a school day. The one good part about it is that the prick teach was trying to give these history notes before Dong, then gave up and tried to start his rap again just as Donny flaked out, and the same with Carlo after lunch. He never did get that history lesson even begun, so we can't have the test Friday.

WINTER 64

I never did write about the time I took my first shot of
heroin. It was about two months back. The funny part
is that I thought heroin was the NON-addictive stuff
and marijuana was addictive. I only found out later what
a dumb ass move it was. Funny, I can remember what
vows I'd made never to touch any of that shit when I
was five or six. Now with all my friends doing it, all kinds
of vows drop out from under me every day. That day
I went down the cellar of Tony's building, all sorts of
characters were in this storage room "shooting gallery,"
cooking up and getting off. I was just gonna sniff a bag
but Tony said I might as well skin pop it. I said OK.
Then Pudgy says, "Well, if you're gonna put a needle
in, you might as well mainline it." I was scared to main,
but I gave in, Pudgy hit it in for me. I did half a fiver
and, shit, what a rush . . . just one long heat wave all
through my body, any ache I had flushed out. You can
never top that first rush, it's like ten orgasms. After a
half hour of nods and slow rapping I shot the rest of
the bag, this time myself. I was high even the next morning waking up. So, as simple as a walk to that cellar, I
lost my virgin veins.

WINTER 64

Ronnie and I took a little busride this evening over to
Alexander's, the giant dept. store over in the Bronx on
Fordham Rd., not too far from my new neighborhood
up here. We wore baggy old coats lifted from our old

men's closets so we could stuff in plenty of goods on this little shopping spree. The job was a snap, we got out of the store and took inventory behind some Navy recruiting office on the Concourse & Fordham and we totalled together about $150 worth of threads. I got a bunch of classy Italian shirts, a pair of striped pants (worn out under my own) and plenty more. Best of the haul was a hip wool turtleneck sweater: $35 in itself. I'll keep that; the import shirts I can get $8 each for them from some spade cat who refers to me as his special wardrobe man. Snap boosting in that place, got to be grade A fish to get busted in there.

So we're all set to pop back on the bus home when one of the most shocking blasts my eyes ever took hit me down. I had to look twice to make sure but there was no doubt about it: smack on the other side of the Navy joint is standing Freddie C., one of the most infamous cats from my old block on the lower east side. I was sure the dudes in the white suits had slammed him into Bellevue for life but there he was, pulling his old trick on the most crowded corner in the Bronx. Yeah, leaning back against the building with one hand running through his hair and the familiar grin over his mug, there he is with his zipper and button wide open slinging his cock around like a lasso with all sorts of poodle walkers, Bronx Jewish mothers with teased up fake blonde hair, Salvation Army lady ringing her bell ten times faster than usual (so it looked like she was keeping time with Freddie) and greasy students staring headon, some gasping, some laughing, and the inevitable three or four making it to call the bulls. Some cat almost fell out of a passing bus yelling if it was a fight he hoped the Irishman would kick the other guy's ass in. Good old Freddie. It was like a piece of the lower east side placed in the Bronx for my benefit. He used to whip that thing out everywhere: train, bus, dance, basketball games (he used to do it as a half time show at the Boys' Club), anywhere you'd name he'd do it, now he's on tour for fuck's sake, the Bronx now, who knows, maybe Westport, Conn. next. One thing I forgot to mention is that it is a worthwhile show, even if you ain't the least queer . . . he's more like a sideshow: that pecker must be a near foot limp . . . no one ever did see it hard, but there was a rumor going around one time that they were playing stickball and the guy before Freddie got mad and busted the bat and just as they were gonna quit he demanded his turn up and hit a homer with . . . well, you guessed it. Just a rumor, that one, but who knows? Well, the cops moved in and that was it for old Freddie C. (If you ain't guessed what the C stands for by now, pack it all in, my man.) It sort of warmed my heart that a regular cat from old 27th St. could draw such a big crowd up in the Bronx. The last laugh came as the crowd broke up and the cop slammed cuffs on Fred before they made him put it back in. The cop reached down toward the giant mass and turned three shades of red as he finally mumbled to the partner that he'd better take off the cuffs a second so Fred could stuff it in. Where the fuck he puts it all I have no idea.

WINTER 64

The other guys in this neighborhood don't seem to be too hip when it comes to smoking grass. Shit, I'm thir-

teen years old and I offered a joint to some nice enough
cats I met that were about sixteen or maybe more and
they almost ran away from me. I was passing by and one
of them recognized me from hanging around the basketball courts and he offered me a beer. These guys
were drinking like fish, so I figure a joint would be in
order to thank him for the beer and, fuck my fanny,
the whole bunch nearly passed out on the spot. It was
the FIRST time any of these four dudes had ever seen
reefer. Shit, I've been smoking it along with all my friends
down on the east side for well over a year . . . (As I said
in a previous diary I had heroin before grass because I
thought grass was the one that hooked you, not scag.
Now since I got the facts straight I only use H once in
a moon.) But these lamebrains thought that grass was
the same as hard stuff. They were even kind of angry
that I was trying to "get them hooked on the first one
for free, and then making them come to me on their
knees giving up all their cash for more." I tried to convince them that the stuff's no habit drug but they wouldn't
hear it and called me a "dope fiend," but they seemed
to cool down a bit and got a little curious and kind of
asked if they could smell it. I handed it to one of them
who told me he read a piece in the paper one time about
a guy throwing his little sister out the window after he
had some of this "marriage-a-wanna." I told them that
all that was a bunch of monkey puke and asked them
how I could be as good as I am in basketball if I was
"hooked," and they admitted that I did have a point. So
while all this bullshit was being flung back and forth,
another friend of theirs, this guy a lot older, comes over.
They introduced me and showed the guy the joint and
the fucking phonies try to show their asses off by saying,

"Want to buy a little marriage-a-wanna, we just had some and it's better than the usual stuff from our other pusher." "Holy cow turd," I thought, "what shit flingers are these lames!"

"Is that weed, wow, I ain't had weed since my army days, how much?"

That put the loudmouths on the spot. They asked the older guy how big a habit he had in the Army.

"HABIT!" the guy laughs. "Who the fuck gets a habit from weed?" I gave the guy a joint . . . free, of course. He thanked me and lit right up. We did two and were zooming. "Wow, this is some fine weed, giggle weed man, check this old bugger's nose walking toward us." I saw the cat he was talking about and went into stitches, my new "dope fiend" pal with me. The other cats saw nothing funny about him, but we were flying and everything around us seemed hilarious. I started to whistle a tune and then the other guy started the same tune not really realizing he was doing it and we both discovered what we were doing after about five minutes (It was probably more like forty seconds but it seemed like five minutes) and we were rolling on the floor, I thought my side would break. Even the other lamos were laughing but they didn't know why. "What the fuck does that stuff do to you?" the guy who offered me the beer asked. "It makes you happy," the old cat says, "and it makes me realize you look like one of them toucans in the Bronx zoo." We both cackled again. The guy did! His nose seemed a foot long! "You hit the head right on the nail," I mumbled by mistake. That was the last straw. We were choking. We had to stumble away from those other guys because they were all gonna call the men with the white suits to take us away. We took one look back and saw

the dumb looks on their faces, "A fucking toucan," the
cat with me shouted waving his hands like Mr. Insanity
himself. We couldn't stop it, I was spitting blood I laughed
so hard. Jesus!

_____ WINTER 64

One of the "fine" Christian Brothers who teaches in this
barb-wire grade school of mine got his cool blown good
today. It seems he pulled his shit once too often. You
see, two days back, as is his way from time to time, he
snagged little Mikey Benavisti cheating on some religion
quiz. As punishment, old brother G. went through his
usual "M.O." This routine, all too familiar to us all by
now, consists of having Mike go behind closed doors in
the coat closet, pull down his trousers and his undies
even, and bend over for a solid ten or so whacks of a
rubber fan belt in the ass. The process always seems to
take an unusually long time . . . Could it be that the good
Brother is deriving some pleasure out of these dutiful
tasks thrust upon him? Mikey finally limps out of the
closet rubbing his hurt and having a bit of trouble when
it comes to sitting. After lunch he showed us the results
in the john and I will tell it to you no bullshit: these were
some real welts, still very visible and already beginning
to blister. These were not the usual joy whacks that fade
in an hour or so . . . "Gonna get the motherfucker," was
all Mikey kept muttering all day.

And next day he damn well did. Right during class,
in the middle of a tense spelling bee, as a matter of fact,
the door bolts open and in storms Mike's big brother

Vinnie, a highly reputed neighborhood tough. Vinnie takes a quick look at Mikey to make sure this is the same dude that put the hurtin' on him, Mikey nods, and Vinnie, no doubt in the mood to kick ass if ever I saw it, proceeds to whip off feeble Bro. G's specks, rips off his holy collar and flings the dude to shit all over the room . . . finally ending it by standing him up against the blackboard and bashing his head on it, making old Bro. G. sort of resemble one of them dolls with the wire necks that you see in the back of people's cars when they're coming home from the amusement park . . . the doll's head just bobbing every which way while the rest of the body is stone stiff . . . "I went to this same school and took beatings, you queer prick, but you didn't do that jive to Mikey out of any 'punishment' . . . so I'm hauling your ass down to the head man and get things straight, now move ass!" The funny thing about this scene was that until Vinnie called the pecker a queer, I never had really thought about it in that light. In fact, a lot of the more lame dudes in this class didn't really know what a homo was at this point (though I certainly had been keyed into that scene already by our coach at the Boys' Club, Lefty, and various other dick snatchers). Now that I thought about it, Brother G. never did pull that closet bit with any ugly guys.

So anyway, Vinnie did see the principal and all but we didn't hear anymore about it yesterday. But today holy Brother G. wasn't there, and by now everybody in the class had learned what Vinnie had meant so we figured that was no doubt the reason why. Actually it made for big talk all day that there we were with a real faggot for our teacher all that time. Guys were running home to their parents and saying, "Heh mom, remember Bro.

G. who you thought was such a nice person always on parents' night? Well guess what. . . ." We asked Mikey if he had heard what became of the bugger but all he knew was he wasn't gonna be back here again. Somebody said they heard one of the other Brothers say something about him going to some special retreat in far off Ithaca.

WINTER 64

My old lady found a nickel bag of grass in my hiding spot under the rug today and flushed it down the toilet. She had a long talk with me and asked me if I was an addict to the stuff. I told her it's heroin you get addicted to, not grass, and I think I finally convinced her. She was not so convinced that she'd give me back the five bucks though, when I asked her for it. In fact I think she got a little angry about it.

SPRING
&
SUMMER
1964

The only good thing about this new neighborhood up here in Inwood is the giant park and the woods. They've got these incredible Indian caves way in deep with all kinds of tunnels and shit you can climb around in. This fat guy got stuck in one the other day and the fire department came and popped him out. It took five big guys pulling on a rope to do it. Funny scene. Up at the caves is this old man every day, name of Bill. He gives out chocolate bars and got this big jug of apple cider we swig on and he plays the flute all day with some weird sound that carries out through the whole woods and a lot of birds come around and squirrels and he tosses breadcrumbs and nuts to them. He's like a saint. My cousin says he's been there since his old man was a little kid. There's one incredibly steep long hill called "Deadman's" that's fantastic for sleigh riding in the winter, but now it's almost summer and in some parts the green is so dense it's like tropical jungles or something. Way up top is a meadow, and past that a cliff overlooking the Hudson. I come up myself and smoke reefer when I have some (can't get it up in this lame place so I get a little off Bunky on 29th when I go down the old neighborhood once in a while) and watch the boats going up along the Palisades. Today I smoked with Willie, the only guy from the school that smokes too, and we watched two jets moving across the sky like it was flat and they were racing on one long strip. I just want to be high and live in these woods. Screw all the rest like Saint Bill down at the caves.

SPRING 64

I did it again tonight after the rest of them had all fallen far asleep. My family that is. I've been doing it for the past week or so everytime I can get some excuse to stay up late, wait, and soft shoe it out. Tonight I just stuck it out in bed, radared the scene and slipped into some baggy jeans, a tee-shirt (stayed barefoot) and went out and up. "Up" is my roof, and what I do is simply take off all my clothes, stand around awhile, a totally naked young boy, stare into the star machine and jerk myself off. Is it strange? Maybe, but it's certainly the most beautiful and exciting way of masturbating I've experienced since I first began my steady practice of the art when I was just turning twelve ... I guess that's almost a year and a half ago now. Time sure flies when you're young and pulling off a lot.

I love it this way. My feet bare against the tar which is soft from the summer heat, the slight breeze that runs across your entire body ... the breezes always seem to hit strongest against my crotch, and you feel an incredible power being naked under a dome of stars while a giant city is dressed and dodging cars all around you five flights down. I guess it has to do with the incredible sexiness of the whole thing, the idea that someone else might pop through the roof door and snag you any second, the possibility of being caught in a situation where there is no possibility of explaining yourself is what is the real turn on ... or that someone is or might be spying on you all the while without a trace.

I got the idea about two weeks ago when I was innocently watching a fire down the street from the roof and I noticed in a top floor window of the building next door a girl about eighteen and juicy standing in front of a huge bedroom mirror naked and playing with herself. (I came in my new grey school pants before I could even get the zipper down and take it out). Needless to mention I spent the entire weekend nights on that same spot, and I eventually got to know her and her pleasures very well in my own little way (she's in her bed alot doing the naked bookworm scene). So after a week of this I decided it would be fun to be on equal terms with her, and I got raw and it turned it into a whole new experience, and a very nice one too.

Now she and I have fallen apart. You might say I got tired of her. I mean I hardly throw a glance to her window anymore . . . it's just better under the big ceiling . . . and it's much more than sex. In fact, I don't really think about anything while I'm in the process of the actual tugging, least of all going into any of the heavy sex fantasies I have to resort to indoors. It's just me and my own naked self and the stars breathing down. And it's beautiful.

SUMMER 64

We had a giant party in the woods last night to celebrate the giant waterpipe that we picked up down in the Village yesterday. Actually, it was only Willie and myself but we had an oz. of grass between us and plenty of beer to drink. This waterpipe was huge, about two feet high, and while we were walking up the steps that lead into the woods some old guy stopped us and looked at the pipe and said, "Now that's an unusual looking contraption, what the hell is it?" "I don't really know," I told him, "I think it's the base to a lamp or something, found it in the garbage can down there, figure I'll take it home and give it to my old lady." "Thatta boy, nice idea, there's hope left for you filthy longhair bastards afterall," and he doddered off walking his dog.

We got to a safe spot and set up the pipe. You got to watch your ass around these woods these days because now the cops got these little motorscooters that take them all around the paths where the cars couldn't go. Only last week a few of my friends tied a wire across the main path down further and the cop did a little unexpected flip that neither he nor the other members of the force around here seemed to appreciate. Hence, there's a lot of balls being busted. But we feel fairly cool in our grassy spot and we toss about a quarter oz. into the pipe for a start. We realize that this was a glutton thing to do but what the fuck. We smoked away and downed a lot of beer. We were getting into digging the arc of an airplane crossing the sky and how it made the sky seem so flat. Since it was dark out and you could just see the red taillights of the planes they were really strange, and they seemed to take an hour to cross from one horizon to the other. There was an old copy of a TV guide under some old leaves next to Willie and we began to goof on the names of certain TV shows like *The Galloping Gourmet*. What the hell is a galloping gourmet for Christ sake? This prompted a laugh fit that lasted quite a while. It was good grass, no doubt about it. And the beer was getting to us too because I felt really woozy. At that point we both started to get tinges of paranoia and every little crackle in the bushes made us freak out and start jumping up ready to check out, so we decided to hide the pipe under some rocks and leaves and pick it up the next day. After we made it back down the steps (it was a fucking difficult trip) we stood around 207th St. goofing with some people we knew and then went down to Forster's, the local bar that all the minors of the neighborhood hang out in. I spent most of the time just drinking beer in the corner and listening to Dylan on the jukebox. The trouble with Forster's is that although half the crowd is guys our own age, the other half is those green horn donkey Irish right off the boat who are nice enough if they ain't too drunk but who are constantly playing the Clancey Brothers and shit like that on the box. So I leave Willie and split really drunk, so stewed in fact that I realize I have to go to work tomorrow selling hot dogs at Yankee Stadium and I'll never make it if I go home and sleep, so I get on the subway and plan to sleep in the park over near the stadium. I swear that the next thing I remember was early morning when some Greeks woke me up and asked me if I could move a little to the side because I was sleeping on their favorite handball court. I looked up and there was Yankee Stadium, but how I made it there and why I fell asleep on the handball court I'll never know. When I walked up to the guy at the desk where the workers go in he told me that I looked disgusting and needed a shave and that I couldn't work. Who the hell needs a shave to sell hot dogs in that horrible place? I caught the subway back and headed straight for the woods to find the waterpipe and when I got there Willie was sitting there turning on some chick. "Where did you go last night?" he asked. "I was playing a little handball," I told him.

SUMMER 64

As far as this summer job of mine at Yankee Stadium goes, I'm a loser all the way. Like you get paid on how much you sell, so these cats hustle their nuts off but I just can't get up for it. Before the game they round up everyone and tell them what they're gonna sell and that's where I get screwed. Like on Friday night, with the whole joint filled with Catholics, I get franks! On the coldest night of the season, overcoat weather, I swear I got ice cream. On the scorching hot days it's a bet I get salty popcorn in the bleachers, never fails. Today was the cake though, like it's bat day and everybody coming in gets a free souvenir bat and I swear on my mother, this son of a bitch got me selling souvenir bats. Any other night, they're a pretty good item, but who's gonna buy one for shit's sake when they're free? I sold two to some kind soul and that's two bucks for the day, so at one eighth commission, I get a big 25¢. Lucky you got to get a minimum of $5.25, but it was a packed house today and most dudes are pulling in $30 for themselves. I've come to a conclusion about what they can do with their fucking job from now on. Next time it's popcorn in sizzling bleachers I'm gonna dump the whole boxful on the outfield and expose myself for all of TV land. So keep your eyes open.

SUMMER 64

Every crowd of young guys has its little games to prove if you're punk or not. My cousin in Newark plays "chickie," which is two cars heading towards each other at about 80 mph. The first driver to swerve out of the way is, of course, the chicken. On the lower east side they'd make you press a lit cigarette onto your arm and have it burn all the way up to the filter without the slightest flinch. Here in upper Manhattan, guys jump off cliffs into the Harlem River, where the water is literally shitty because right nearby are the giant sewer deposits where about half a million toilets empty their goods daily. You had to time each jump, in fact, with the "shit lines" as they flowed by. That is, there were these lines of water crammed with shit along the surface about five feet long that would come by once every forty seconds. So you had to time your jump in between the lines just like those jitterbugs down in Acapulco got to time their jumps so they hit the water just as the wave is beginning to break.

It was also a big thrill and a standard joke whenever a really giant scumbag floated by. Man, did we see some whoppers: the people in this sewer district sure have big dicks. One time we even saw a dead pig float by (the animal, that is). He must have come off the Hudson from upstate, freed himself from a livestock barge and drowned maybe. It was scary white and jelly-like, bloated to double its normal size. I remember the sight of it cruising by and (really) no one swam for about three days.

So today we met in the park near the basketball courts,

Johnny, Danny, and I, played a few quick games, downed a couple of beers, and headed up the street. (Seamen Ave. is the name of the street, in fact, pretty funny name; and I actually know a chick who lives on the corner of Seamen and Cumming Streets, who fucks her weight in guys, but living on a corner with names like that, who could blame her.) Well, we walked our way up to the 225th Street bridge, cross over into the Bronx, shimmy to get down to the railroad tracks to get down to the cut (which is the name of a huge rock you jump off). Meanwhile, on the way, we're chased by the huge watchdog, a ferocious German Shepherd, and we had to run our balls off and climb over another fence to avoid it. So we made it for a change because sometimes we're not so lucky with that mutt and it will tear the leg of your pants off in one chomp, perhaps a good part of your ass with it. One day we were with Sam McGiggle and he couldn't make it to the fence in time so we told him to freeze perfectly still and the dog wouldn't bother him. So he statued himself in some insane position and the mutt came up to him, sort of sniffed at him for a second or two, and just as old Sam felt relieved, it bit him accordingly right square in the bum-bum.

Well, we made it to the cut and poked around the bushes at the base to find our hidden swim suits and jocks (since there were no lockers this was the next best thing). Then we buried our money in the safest spot, and began to change. Just down to our scivvies, we hear giggles shooting up from behind the bushes and wheel around to find three chicks there trying to dig on the show. No other solution, we saw, but to attack, so we whip off our underwear and charge after them, totally naked and slinging jocks around in our hands. Their true purity exposed, they were off in the breeze, giggling and peeking back now and then at our free swinging tools. On go our suits and we begin to ascend the cut. The cut is actually only about twelve feet wide, with the Harlem River on one side, and the Hudson-Harlem train line tracks in the rear. It has a series of minor cliffs to jump off, and they gradually get higher until you reach the top, about eighty-five feet. Every plateau you jump has its own separate name like Suicide and Hell's Gate, Angel's Toe and the top, the élite goal that all this bullshit is about, Hell's Angel.

That's where we were, the very top, flat solid rock which is cracked in parts so that small clover-like plants grow out of the crevices. We sat tense, waiting for the sightseeing boat, The Circle Line, to make the turn around the bend down near the bridge and head toward us. That was what really made the jump worthwhile, with all the lame couples like old tourists from Ohio, and nuns, and Japanese executives, and other odd N.Y.C. visitors who got fished into paying five beans to sail around the island, watching us go down into the stinking water. Well, Danny was the first, Johnny and I peering over the edge as he made it clear over the first and only obstacle, a small tree that shot out of the rock about five feet below, then straight ahead, hands close at sides, body stiff, and feet locked tightly, hitting the surface missile-like. From up there it seemed like 50008 feet to the bottom. But Danny had jumped Hell's Angel before, so it was old hat to him, but now it was John's turn, and he, like me, was a rookie at the top. Scared shit and mouth wide, he peeped one more time onto the river, waved at the waiting sightseers, took one step back, five hundred deep breaths, muttered, "Fuck it," then yelled out the same thing, clutched his balls with both hands and jumped. Down he was going, legs spread far apart, and jitterbugging like he was doing the Popeye or something, still firmly clutching his crotch. "Bad form," I sighed, as he hit the water, and what a fucking understatement that was. It was pitiful, he hit the water like a fucking octopus, limbs flying everywhere, and the splash contained a smacking sound that hurt all the way up to me at the top of the cliff. When he came up to the surface he swam to the shore with one hand paddling and holding his sore, sore ass with the other, so that he was slow enough to get attacked by a fair sized shit line, the whole fucking scene having Danny in stitches over on the shore near the tracks. My turn now, the boat almost past, all the people at attention yelling for me to do it, the sadistic bastards.

I didn't really think, I didn't even take my sneakers off, I just jumped into this jerky dream that lasted all the way down until I hit bottom. The feeling isn't movement anyway, but rather being suspended in front of the sheer cliff, mid-air, with the waters rising up sharp and fast at you. I hit water hard, but I didn't go too deep, coming up to see all the sightseers applauding. Then I swam to shore to meet the others and we turned, pulled down our shorts, and flashed our moons to the old sightseeing buggers as the boat pulled away and headed for the Hudson. We got dressed and went back (Eddie the old queer peeking into the bushes as we changed, by the way). I got back to the neighborhood and decided to go home to eat and write and sleep; I know I can always wait till tomorrow to go around and brag and let everyone know what a big shit I am and all that.

SUMMER 64

I was drinking tonight in the park with Danny, Fat Eddie and Sean so we got stewed out and decide to break into the Park house to clip a few basketballs for warmups in our big game next week at Long Beach. Actually, we're not really breaking in since Danny robbed the key yesterday from Sal, the dumb park attendant when he left it in the door as he was cleaning up the bathroom. Sal is incredible. He worships the devil or some crazy thing like that and he often kneels over the toilet as he cleans up the john at the end of the day and starts praying with crazy chants and freaky grunts, a real loulou. So we sneak over to the park house, open the door and break open the equipment closet with the handy crow bar on the tool rack. We got four brand new Bob Cousy model balls, tucked them into a canvas bag and split the park and left them in a safe spot in Danny's house. We told his mother that we won them in the St. Jude's Church bazaar through an incredible lucky coincidence. Then we go back to the park, sit around on the benches outside the courts totally wiped out. Suddenly a cop car comes tooling in pretty fast and right at us. We panic and take off toward the giant ball fields. I move my ass left, straight across the field and, as I might have guessed, everyone else heads to a hideout in the small set of bleachers at the right. Cops follow (of course) me, so I tear my balls full speed ahead but now I'm trapped right in a flood light following my every step and the car itself closing in. I can hear the other hardons watching me like an idiot and laughing out loud. I looked like I was doing the "James Brown" they told me later. I'm almost making it to the other end of the field by now and I can ditch them from there, when I hear an unpleasant, "Stop, or I'll put a bullet in your leg." I stop right there, no doubts. The man pulls up next to me, one gets out, shoves me up to the car and says to some joker who I notice in the back seat of the car, "Is this the guy?" "Hmmm, what guy?" and out of the car steps Leapy Louie Salvadorio, big basketball rival of mine from the Bronx and the son of my barber, Sal Salvadorio. "No," says Louie, "this is Jim Carroll, big basketball rival of mine from here in Manhattan." It seems Louie got taken off around here tonight and he's been cruising with the man to catch the dude. The cop asks me how come I was running away so I told him that I ran because all the others ran. "Dopey!" he says to me, and whacks me good across the knees with his billie-bat for busting his balls with the dumb chase. I went back to all the other wise asses and they were cracking on me and imitating my Charlie Chaplin run all night. Fuck them, and fuck Sal the Barber and his shitty haircuts from now on too.

SUMMER 64

I got canned from my shitty job at Yankee Stadium tonight and I couldn't care less. As usual I got the worst product in the joint to hustle: ice cream. Not that ice cream is the worst in general, popcorn is the general bummer; but tonight was about 20 degrees and drizzly out, and even the fruits in this place ain't that fruity. So I'm going through the usual motions in the upper deck, only good thing happening was this blonde in section 20 throwing this gigantic spread a few rows up, perfect eye-to-beaver position. Black panties and all. Then the rain lets go harder and the ground crew shuffles out and covers the field with the field coverer, or whatever the hell they call it, while all the saps in the upper deck tear ass back to the very top rows where the rain is blocked out. I head up too and two chicks call me over for a sale. I knew it could not be just the ice cream they wanted so I sit down and rap. Turns out they smoke grass and all, or so they say, and I'm getting on o.k. with them, having a smoke and sitting back without that fucking ice box on my back. Then along comes Mr. Balls-buster himself, Rudy the foreman. This prick sneaks constantly around the ballpark checking up on dudes goofing off and I'm one of his prize targets. He's a real kraut who no doubt would have made a great shower room commander in any of Hitler's war camps. This time he got me clean, busting about ten regulations, but sitting on the job is the absolute no-no. Only one hope, I leave the box there and try to make a run for it, hoping he can't make out my face or badge number if I can make it down to the lower deck. It's an extra added attraction for the fans and the whole upper deck is cheering me on to out run the Kaiser in this ridiculous scene. Finally I shoot down a ramp to make my break but it's wash-up time for me 'cause the ramp is closed and I'm snagged cold. Prick face rips off my badge in this fucking pompous gesture like he was taking back my medal of honor and orders me to get the ice cream. I tell him all about what he can do about getting the ice cream back and just turn and bop out of the joint, costume on and all and I ain't never going back to that fucking hole with its six million ramps and stair cases again, Yeah Yankees!

SUMMER 64

Willie Coll and I arrived in the Long Beach station at about 3:30. Tonight was the first in the big playoff series in the festive Long Beach Chamber of Commerce Summer Basketball Tournament: Junior, Senior, and Pro divisions. We are in the Senior division, and during the regular season we had lost only one game against Orlando's Furniture Store. Our team is from Shine's Bar and Grill. Our opponent tonight is St. Mary's Holy Roman Lions. When we went to eat the terrible pizza in this place called the "Patio Chef" we encountered a few little pricks who were goofing on our long hair. One bastard snuck up and poured ketchup in Willie's hair and Willie threw his pizza in the guy's face. A quick little fight broke out between these two people and some big guy who had seen us play basketball down there before, broke up everything and explained to the other fuck that Willie and I were the stars of the basketball league down at the recreation center. "I didn't know faggots like you could play basketball," he said, "I'm sorry." Willie's mouth was bleeding from a punch. "Here, wash it out with this soda," said the guy who punched him. Willie took one sip of the soda, slipped in (and this is true) 200 mgs. of pure crystal amphetamine and gave it back to the prick, who drank the rest. Then we left for the beach to wash the ketchup out of Willie's hair.

We won the game easily, so in two nights we would play Orlando's furniture store for the championship. After the game, the infamous queer college scout Benny Greenbaum comes creeping around the dressing room. Tom McNulty, our center, tells Benny he can blow him in front of everyone for $15. "Can't put out the money until I see the meat," says Benny. Tom takes out his cock, at least seven inches long, and Benny swallows about fifteen gulps of the fresh Long Beach air while his eyes flash the great quick-sale sign. What humorous disgust when Benny started lapping. Tommy got his money and we left. I'm going to fuck every teenage girl in Long Beach tonight.

We go to Tom Miggrello's house for a party. When we get there Tom is out, so we go inside and get drunk while we wait. When we run out of beer Danny and Ronny go out to get some more. They get back in a few minutes and tell us about the bastard who tried to rob their beer and how they beat him up. Just then Tom walks in the door with his clothes half torn off: he was the one that Ronny and Danny beat up. "This is Tom," I said. "And these are the two pricks that just beat my ass in," said Tom. Eventually we got it squared away and everybody got drunk. I fell down the stairs one time I was so drunk. I called up my mother and she said, "You're drunk."

SUMMER 64

Tonight still in Long Beach we got drunk, but not as bad as last night, so we went over to some terrible bar and tried to pick something up. A guy told us that the Celia sisters were heading down toward the beach. I had gotten a blow job once from Alice Celia and her little sister had quite a reputation herself, so Willie and I headed after them. When we caught up to them we waited about ten feet behind and watched them duck into an alleyway—they were both stone drunk. When we passed by we saw them making out with each other all over the concrete. "Boy, that really turns me on," Willie said to me, then he called for Alice and she came over and said to me, "I remember you, you came in my mouth and it tasted like strawberries." This girl is really fucked up, I thought. She was only fourteen too; her sister was thirteen. "Want to go down to the beach with us?" I asked.

On the way to the beach Alice pissed right in the street. But I don't want to soil my diary with a description of that. Then some other guys spotted us with them and told some other guys who told some other guys and I swear before long the whole fucking town was on the beach waiting for blow jobs. One guy came up to me and asked what was going on. "These two girls I think are about to give out an awful lot of blow jobs," I said. "Get in line," someone else told him. Willie and I left that fucking scene, got a ball, and went down to the courts in the dark to practice foul shots for the game tomorrow.

SUMMER 64

We were all over at the Catholic school's youth night last night playing a little ball and the old guy that was in charge, some jerkoff priest who's hung up on being a priest, had to cut out early so he trusted the keys to the place to Donny and told him to lock up when we were finished. Well we did that and all, but today we had a great idea to have an extra set of keys made for our own convenience before we gave them back. So we all stop off at the hardware store on the way down to the poolroom and get a duplicate of each key. At the dance tonight we're all sitting around drunk and we get word of this big party that the local American Legion is going to have in the school in a week or two and that they got about ten cases of whiskey stashed away in the kitchen plus uncountable cases of beer. It doesn't take long for us to decide that tonight is the perfect night to put our new keys to use and get ourselves a free supply of good booze. We wait around after the dance and give everyone a chance to clean up and get their asses out and then about four of us sneak to the side door and let ourselves in. It was a tense scene, but in about half an hour there was a minor parade of ourselves transporting four cases of liquor and six cases of beer over to the woods of Inwood park and finding some nice safe spot for our little treasure. Since we discover a nice cool stream, the beer is cold in no time and we polish off two of the cases right there on the spot. And since we have almost fifty quarts of whiskey in our hands now I can forsee an awful lot of drunk sons of bitches in the next few months, and that for sure includes me. And I'm sure we couldn't have picked a nicer bunch of guys to rob than those pricks in the American Legion.

SUMMER 64

Out here in Long Beach, Long Island again, not really playing in any basketball summer league or anything, just visiting Fat Eddie from 28th Street whose family has a bungalow out here. Drank two bottles of Codeine cough syrup on the way out in the train's bathroom so I didn't mind making that boring trip by myself, did the entire trip in fact on one long nod, such a dynamite head that I almost stayed on the train when we reached the Long Beach stop, which wouldn't have been too cool, considering that's the last stop on the line and I don't dig spending nights in some fucking freightyard out on some L.I. marsh. A good medicine head can even top junk some days though of course there's no rush or shit but you get fucked-up all the same. So I mad dash off the train and head over to catch the bus that will take me to the other end of the beach where Fattie lives. I was trying to cop a short nod again on the bus ride but this crazy old lady keeps giving me shit about being a commie because I got a red tee-shirt on (if she looked harder the dumb bitch would have seen it had "GOOD SHEPHERD FALCONS" right across the front of it) but she goes on insisting that she has this vision that I'm gonna die within a month because a giant clock was gonna fall on my head. Total fruit, they always got to pick on me. So finally I tell her to fuck off but she keeps on screaming and I get such a fucking headache that I got to get off the bus, totally brought down. When I finally got to his dump of a house, Fattie was sitting upstairs smoking hash with these incredible blonde twins. "This is Winkie and this is Blinkie and, Winkie and Blinkie, this is Jim." "I saw you in the big championship game last week," Winkie says, "I like you." Great. They, Winkie and Blinkie, were exact lookalikes with very sexy Grande Concourse Jewish features like with all that pink gloss lipstick and teased up hair and enormous tits that hung out of the blouses about six inches from my stoned face.

They both had on very tight blue jean shorts that were cut up to make them even more tempty. Blinkie got up and passed me the pipe and I took a toke or two and freaked it to Eddie and flopped on the mattress next to Blinkie and nodded out with my head on her lap. I perceived sexual overtones creeping about, so I figured I better go into the bathroom and throw up the medicine to bring me down a bit, in order to get it up a lot and I did and I was pretty straight within an hour or so and hip on getting together with a scene or two. Then it was about an hour more of smoking the hash with my head on Blinkie's lap with an occasional grab for one of her titty treats. I was feeling pretty bored by then and anxious to fuck her until they ordered the ambulance. Then the ice broke, if that's what you want to call it, and Winkie popped up and began to grind around and unbutton, rather slip off, more or less, the top buttons of her low cut blouse, and I eventually got a goodo peek at those perky knocks flying out of a tiny tiger striped bra. Then she struggled, but finally managed to get the shorts down revealing just some teenie panties with an out of sight leather fringe around them. I was wishing at this point that I decided to lay on *her* cunt instead of Blinkie's but then I got this obvious notion and unbuttoned Blinkie's blouse and slipped off her bottoms and, you guessed it, they were identical as ever. Then the bras came off, nice abstract sucked often nipples. "Like that?" Blinkie inquired. "You have very nice tits and I am going to squeeze them right now," I told her. Then I squeezed them, then a few circles around the outer part of the nipple and then my tongue, hard flat licks over the entire nipple, tongue tip lightly in circles on tit tip, varieties of various tiny bites and sucks etc, etc. We got up and found a more colorful room because I like to fuck in faintly colorful rooms. Then she rolled onto the bed in the other room giggling while I stood at the door, going through my usual this is great but can I handle the fucking nympho bit, and she was really younger than me like about 13 or so. So I started down with my blue jeans and tossed them over the bedpost, nice bed, old but really large and low, and a low blue light on in the corner to boot. I didn't have any underwear on, it was at half mast now, getting bigger by the second. "You have a nice cock," she spoke, a witless remark for the present situation. "If I rub it on this nice pussy of mine will it get larger and larger?" She dangled the panties down her legs and off and began to fiddle her clit. She was right. She was right, I was really up, she could have done chin ups on the fucking thing it was so hard. I knelt onto the bed and started with her feet and worked snake tongue up to her puss. (She was that type, I knew for some reason.) I worked on the thing for a good ten minutes and then wormed my way to her hot mouth and swung it around in there for a good while. This was a hot chick by now, she was grabbing for the prick like nutty. "Don't go too much on it, I want to make this thing last." She winked at that. Corny, yes, but all-American and a new turn on. Little Blinkie had just turned from pure Bronx poodle walking slut to Kansas Central cheerleader. Then I laid over and let her do a little mouth work on it, bigger than I ever saw it in all my fifteen years, let me tell you, I was proud of its showing. The sucking felt great, it also gave me a chance to jiggle those monster tits for awhile too. It's wonderful the way a pair like that feels when a chick's body is bent over on her knees like that. Then I asked to get in on it so I moved around so her cunt was above me, lightly over the clito at first then in and out of her wet hole, outoffuckingsight. Her pubic hair a deep black, nice contrast to her blonde beehive job upstairs. Up to here I was holding back all I could, but then I moved her away and put her down on her knees and shoved it all in from behind at first, getting a great grip on her thighs and guiding her. Then turned her over and shoved her legs up as far as I could, tight grip, really, really tight, then slowly in and out then to our sides so that the bone above my thing was rubbing her clit, out again teasing her clit, an occasional nod or two from the Codeine for comic relief, then bang faster and faster and my finger tickling her sweet ass . . . a simple All-Midwest Conference lay in truth, but worth laying down here nonetheless, and pump, pump . . . bingo COME TIME (Ah, just like a can of spinach to old Popeye). I could have filled a motherfucking bucket with all that sap. Laid there awhile with her, can never get over the drag of that fucking bit, tried to squeeze a last nod or two, watched her roll the basketball that was in the corner over her body, then I did it for a little while to her, made her hump on it, turn around and at the door, Winkie! "Time to go home sweetheart," she reminded Blink. So she got up and put her things on and stared, "Come over to our place in the afternoon tomorrow, that was fun, OK?" Sure bet, sure bet. They split. Fat Eddie came into the room. He looked like he just sweated off about forty fucking pounds. We smoked some more and decided we should get some sleep. "What do you think of Winkie and Blinkie?" he asked. "I think they're fucking great," I told him.

FALL 64

FALL 64

It's my first day at the ultra-rich private school that I
got a scholarship to come to. I had a hard time trying
to figure out what I was doing there, and I got funny
looks from everyone and thought how funny it was all
those Jewish kids singing away those old Christian tunes
like that at the chapel service in the morning. Some
teacher in back of me kept poking on my shoulder to
get me to sing but I just sat there with a bored look on
my face. Before the first class I spoke with a nice enough
little guy named Eggie Blaumgarden, whose old man
owns a big diamond cutting firm, very impressive to me.
It turns out that he's a great tennis star (sixth in the East
for his age) and he's interested in art. "Got a few Renoirs
over at my place," he lays on me, "come over for dinner
some time and check 'em out." Sure thing Eggie. Then
I got into hot water with Mr. Brothers, fancy Oxford
graduate Latin teacher, who freaks out when I answer
a question "Yah" instead of "Yes, sir." He keeps me after
class and explains how he understands, with mounds of
sympathy, how my family are lowly slobs and all but to
discipline myself to proper replies and other classroom
etiquette. Sure thing. Then at lunch the headmaster,
Mr. Belt, comes over and sits at my table and tells me
that my hand should be removed from sight while dining. I thought he meant the hand that I held the fork
with, so I sat there for half a minute puzzled until I
realized it was the other hand he was talking about. He's
an overly sincere type guy, you know the kind, like a
politician, they always wind up screwing you sooner or
later. Frankly I don't dig the guy. I feel like farting and
blowing up the 257 years of fine tradition of this place.

After lunch I spent a little time in the school trophy room, which is actually a sort of lounge where there are fancy v-shaped sofas and all that and a walnut cabinet with all the school's trophies in it (not many, I might add, in fact, I've got more trophies at home than this place got in 257 years). So I'm minding my own business reading *Time* magazine when some guy from my own class, Larry Labratory, I think his name is, tries to insist that he was reading the magazine first. "Nice try there, champ," I say, "but I've been sitting here ten minutes now, you see?" So, can you picture this, he actually tries to take the thing from me, the prick, and for lack of a more peaceful solution, I get up and punch him out. His nose bleeding, he gets up and whimpers off, prob- ably to squeak to some teacher. Sure enough, he's back in two minutes, with some old man from the History Dept., pointing dead at me, a handkerchief held up to his bleeding mug. It was only the testimony on my behalf by Eggie Blaumgarden that saved me from getting into a big hassle and being sent down to Mr. Bluster, our principal. Everyone seemed to hate that guy Larry Labratory anyway, so I drew a little applause from the lounge clique when the history guy shook off.

After boring afternoon History classes, I decided to hang around a while and watch the football team work out. Strictly lame, let me tell you, I could round up any ten friends of mine from downtown or uptown and whip their asses. Some senior asked me to hold the ball for him while he practiced field goals, thinking I was just another jerk-ass freshman. I did, and this guy kicked the thing like it was a bag of shit or something. I say, "Let me try one," and he says OK, thinking he's doing this little punk a big favor. I stepped back, took two

strides forward, and breezed one over from 32 yards
(this is in loafers, don't forget) and the guy just knelt
there with his mouth hung open. I thought his jock
would fall off and roll right down the leg of his clean
little uniform. Then I tipped off to the subway, secretly
loving everything about this crazy place.

FALL 64

I went back down the old neighborhood today, had to
go to the wake of this old friend of mine, Bobby Sachs.
I planned to make it downtown earlier to visit some
people but got hung up at school cleaning desks and
shit for cutting out once too often. This drag clean-up
lasts until 4:30, though to tell the truth I didn't do a lick
of work 'cause some dumbie was in charge and I hung
out in the bathroom all the while and read about that
wise-ass dwarf Alexander Pope. I wasn't missed and signed
out with the rest of the crew on time. I made it down
to the funeral place about five and there must have been
every guy from 29th to 14th St. there. I talked to all
these old friends for half an hour just as a cover 'cause
I was trying to avoid having to look at Bob's dead body
in the center of the room. I never saw a body in a casket
in my life, even at my grandmom's wake my parents
didn't make me go.

Bobby died of leukemia. He got it two years ago but
had such a strong body (he was always the best at sports)
that he kept fighting it off. They gave him six months
at first, then he turned a trick and got better . . . even
got out for awhile, though it was a different person when

you saw him, then he went back in a year ago, like his brother was telling me, the line on his hospital chart just fell straight down in a perfect angle. I looked at his body and it was death for the first time in my life. His face was thin and wrinkled, almost ape-like, his hair just grey patches on his scalp. He looked sixty years old, and he was sixteen. I couldn't believe how skinny his arms were . . . it was like having the skeleton of someone you knew put in front of you.

I left dazed out in the streets like I had just come out of a four hour movie I didn't understand. I thought about that face all night, and death. I almost flipped and I took two reds even to knock me out but they don't feel like they're working.

FALL 64

The posh private school I go to is only a few blocks away from Central Park. Consequently, in the warmer part of the fall we have gym periods in the park consisting mainly of touch football. It's nice in a way to get to spend an hour in the park playing ball twice a week but the bullshit end of the stick is the walk over there in your corny ass little gym shorts and white tee-shirts. It doesn't bother the rest of the lames in my freshman class but personally I don't dig the shit you take from the black cats and PRs that live in the neighborhood, their whis-tling and what not, calling us all rich little faggots . . . Dig it, I could bust the ass off any of those dudes woofing at us from the public basketball courts on Amsterdam if it was worth my time, but lately I've been wearing blue jeans over instead of that other shit and lagging behind all the other kids, so everything is cool, as long as the headmaster don't catch an eye of me and give me another lecture on the "rules" of the school. Fuck dumb rules, let me wear what I want . . . No trouble from Mr. Doolittle, the cat that runs the phys. ed. here because he's the basketball coach too and he never gives me any hassles.

But today when we got in the park, I laid back from the rest and got high on a little reefer walking along the horse trail, I get to the field and start playing and I'm stoned and goofing on the whole scene but digging the game too, though my coordination was a little off level. So anyway I finished up and he toots his little whistle and time to get back for boring Latin class. Not too boring today though I figure because I still got a good half reefer left and I lag back again, squat in a patch of bushes and light up to make my man Virgil a little more interesting. All is cool, but all is not cool for long. I hear a sudden hoofing sound heading my way full blast and I know it ain't no Lone Ranger and Tonto. Fuck! It's two horse-patrol cops giddy-apping right into the goddamn bushes. I toss the joint in back of me pronto just as one cop is off his horse and standing right in front of me in a fucking clump of bushes. . . . "What the hell you in here for, you punkbastard, I think we got a good idea." I looked at the guy, wrecked out of my brain, and tell him I was sneaking a smoke before I went back to school after my gym class out here. The cop asks me where my teacher is but they're probably back at the school by now so that's what I tell the man. He tells me to get out of the bushes and I figure shit, lucky he ain't looking for the joint, but then in that case what the fuck do they think I was doing, beating off or something? We're in the open now and he says to his partner something about me fitting the description. I look up at the other cat on his horse still and, holy duck fuck, it's my little league coach from the old neighborhood, Steve Malone. "JIM?" He almost falls off the goddamn horse. "What the hell are you doing?" I tell him in stoned dialogue, "School down block ... go ... play ball class ... gym, you know ... smoke ... sneak behind ... high Steve, good to see yer." I realize it was total gibberish and try to start again but he breaks in and tells me not to sound so nervous, that they were looking for some guy who molested some little girl the other day in the bushes around there and he had red hair so they did a charge when they saw me, then he nods to his partner and tells him who I am ... In fact, he goes on telling him about the no-hitter I pitched to win our team the championship and all and starts bragging about the smart move he made in that game having a guy steal third who later got in on a sacrifice etc. I'm looking at the guy blasted out still thinking about the grass and he's blabbing about weirdos raping kids, winding up with a description of the speech he made at the League dinner for winning coach of the year. I was also missing half my class in Latin. I tell him finally I gotta go back to school and he just nods and waves a tiny gesture and keeps on rambling about goddamn baseball to the other guy who is all ears and starting to tell Steve about his own coaching experiences out in Flatbush or some fucking place. I get into Latin just before the bell rings and put on a fake limp coming in telling him I got hurt in gym and had to see the nurse. He swallowed it in a vague kind of way.

FALL 64

Today at school we had our annual Thanksgiving fast for the benefit of the poor and hungry blacks we hear of scattered throughout the South. Anyone who sympathizes with the injustice of poverty in the South does not eat his meal as a symbol of this injustice. I'm sure it interests a starving black in Mississippi that I am not eating my lunch today. Frankly, I was too embarrassed to be the only cat in the school to eat his meal so I snuck down to the corner and copped a cheeseburger. Symbolic gestures are certainly self-satisfying but they are not too nourishing for anyone anywhere. Somebody is conning everyone else and themselves with plain dumb ideas as performed here today. What happens to the food they prepared today? All that turkey and mashed potatoes would probably seem pretty dried out if we shipped it down South, even by air mail. It would have been interesting to point out that there are a lot of hungry dudes walking down Columbus Ave. that could have dug a free meal. But some of them might be drug addicts and shit and they'd no doubt make a big mess of the lunch room that all the black cleaning women would have a hard time cleaning up. I suggest that tomorrow somebody symbolically stick a stale drum stick of today's lunch up the ass of whoever was humane enough to organize this farce.

FALL 64

My friend from school, that die-hard Marxist Bunty
Gargen, fixed me up on an afternoon blind date with a
friend of his big titted girlfriend to see some old Bogart
movies down on Bleecker St. Bogart, by the way, went
to our school for three years but got the boot for bad
grades. But aside from that little fact we met at his chick's
pad 'cause her folks were on the fly and there I got to
meet Melody, my chick for the day and what a strange
one. Not bad looking you see . . . just strange, about five
feet tall, a little plump, long hair with a round face
which, with her huge eyes, made her look like an antique
doll. She had a fixed weird stare that reminded me of
one of those little kids in that flick, *Village of the Damned*.
One thing I noticed right off: she had the biggest pair
of knockers for a girl of fourteen that I ever saw. Those
jugs looked like melons. So, of course, she too is heavy
with the Marx bag, work shirt and blue jeans (standard
outfit) . . . can spot 'em a mile off. Another weird thing
was that on the way down to the flick she asked me if I
"took pot" and from the tone she used I figured to say
"no," and did, and good thing 'cause she started to run
down how those people "Do strange things at times,"
and shit like that which she read about in *Life* or someplace where they take the new drugs and make them
seem horrible demons for the dumbass public. I can see
her being wary of acid 'cause of that crap-writing but
grass? I had some on me in fact, I figured all them folks
on that scene were into smoke. Then another strange
move, in the movies I put my goddamn arm around her
and she brushes it off and mumbles, "There's a time
and a place for everything." Jesus, what people my age

go to the movies to watch a movie? But so much for that and I dig old Bogey anyhow. On the way back to the apartment I put my arm around her again and the same sliding hand and the same shit reply. "There's a . . ." I had thought I had this type nailed on the head like at peace marches and shit I've picked up many a rich young commie and almost got raped by them. But this chick, shit . . . this chick with them gorgeous boobs right there bouncing, and no go. I was getting pissed off, it was gonna be a waste of the day, shit, fucking Bunty, I felt like making his gig. Fuck! I even paid her way into the show: a breakthrough in my image. Then we get back to the house and we're digging these Dylan sides and in a flash she boobs her way over and whispers that we should go into one of the bedrooms. Big shit . . . I figured another theory on DAS CAPITAL, but that drag is usually after the nooky is over. Before I know it she got me down on the bed with my zipper open and my whole hand up her precocious snatch. She was the most far out antique doll you'd ever want to meet. In the clinch she giggles, "See, there's a time and a place for everything and this is the time."

WINTER 1965

Took in a Knicks game at the Garden tonight with
Kevin Dolon, Yogi, his beastly chick Muffy, and Nardo
Poo. Knicks beat the Celtics for the first time in two
years, the old cigar chomping Garden regulars were
going ape from their regular balcony hangouts. They
love to see Bill Russell have a bad game and, fuck, they
really got down on that cat's back and poor Russell did
have a rare screwed game tonight. He wasn't standing
out at all on defense. In fact, he was sheer shit. Good
old Johnny Green was snatching rebound after rebound
over him, and he was particularly bad shooting. Like
the dude never was a good shooter, but tonight he was
hideous. At one point near the end he was all but a foot
from the basket when some drunk hack yelled out "Shoot,
yer got the wind with yer, yer bum." I could even make
out a few saps on the Celts bench cracking on that one.
You know the Knicks ought to hand me a free pass for
all the home games. Like honest, here I've been to nine-
teen home games in the last two years and they won
every fucking one . . . and they continue to wind up in
last place each year. I swear this on me mom's grave . . .
or make it me grandma's grave 'cause my moms is still
alive.

But the funny part about tonight was the ride home.
We made use of the crowd of course to sneak under the
turnstile for freebies, then after a long wait the dumpy
uptown local chugs in. These locals are the ultimate for
lousy transit. They break down every other stop and
move like they ran on flashlight batteries. I got in one
relic last week and the fucking seat broke in half when

I sat down to a chorus of laughs from the other jerks riding it. I picked up a paper and it was dated 1959 . . . that means it's at least four years since they swept the wreck. So when this one's doors open it's every sap for himself and after a mad dash, me, Muffy, Yogi and Poo grab seats, Kevin didn't make it and he's there getting crushed and swinging on the bars. Seemed like the entire Garden was in the car, fucking Sardineville. Small miracle, the tinker got started. Then some strange giggles start up, mostly the people around us. Soon all through the car heads start popping over other heads and total hysterics. I notice all eyes on Kevin, jokers down the other end even pointing at him. We look up and see why. Here he is swinging like an ape with his zipper full down and his entire cock hanging like a clock. He's just swinging away, not a bit aware of any of this, whole wang in the breeze. Nardo Poo breaks silence by looking at him and tactlessly banging out a crack about he never thought Irishmen were that big. Muffy is there pulling that famous old girl trick like she ain't looking but got a four-inch space between each finger with her hands over her eyes. Kevin looks down and turns nine shades of lobster. So just as he tries to tuck it in like nobody saw him (sure thing, Kev) this transit cop is there insisting he's a pervert doing the shit on purpose. Finally this little old lady stumbles up and tells the cop it was all an accident, so fuzz tips but the whole train is still goofing on Kev. Lucky for him we got off next stop to catch the express. Dolon just sat with his head down the whole way uptown.

WINTER 65

Today was our first game of the season against a very lame squad from St. Hilda's. This pushover has two advantages: easy win to boost morale, and the fact that they always bring busloads of very foxy chicks along with them. Hence every time I'd dunk a ball in the warmups or made an impressive play the chicks in the stands let out a bunch of "oohs" and "ahhs" and seemed to throw a leg spread that increased to a wider and wider position in direct proportion to each "ooh" that by the time I dunked one backwards I could almost distinguish what color panties each chick sitting there was wearing as I peeked over coming down the court. These are the fans that bring out a player's true inspiration, though with all those beavers flashing it did ruin one's concentration a bit.

So we're up by twenty at half and I got about eighteen points. I came back out to pull some fancy-ass passes and dribbling to show off in the second half but instead I wound up embarrassing the shit out of myself. Everything is cool until I go up to block some cat's layup on a fast break and I hear a giant rippp . . . between my legs. I look down but don't notice a thing until I start dribbling downcourt. The entire gym is in stitches. I'm dribbling fast and peek down to discover the entire crotch of my pants is ripped apart and they were like a skirt . . . nothing holding them from beneath! The shorts are bobbing up and down and my total ass (since all I've got under 'em is a jock) is totally exposed on each bob up. I passed to Marc and tried to call time but nobody saw me and they had the ball and it took another thirty seconds more of my little peek show before Anton Neu-

tron got a rebound and I called time. The coach, serious
Dudley Doolittle, was even laughing, a first in his career
I think. So he sends me downstairs with the manager to
get another pair and I trot to the exit blushing face and
blushing ass. Everyone pointing and goofing, I stop near
the exit, bend over, and throw a giant moon . . . I left,
a slight pink, through the exit with the whole gym giving
me a mock standing ovation.

WINTER 65

I've been hanging around lately, with all the other heads
in this dreary neighborhood, at this place called "Headquarters," which is actually just the apartment of two
friends of mine, Brian and John Browning. It's an amazing place where there are usually anywhere between ten
and thirty locals hanging out either laughing insanely
from grass fits or simply on the nod from smack. I've
lived here from time to time when my parents gave me
the toss, and woke up here this morning, in fact, after
a huge hash goof last night. There were about twelve
other dudes out on the floor when we got each other
up for early bird cartoons and the remainder of the
hash. Sloppy Eddie wandered in with a case of milk and
thirty-six loaves of bread that he and Willie Appleears
clipped from the Grand Union down the block before
they opened. Since this is supposed to be a quiet, middle-
class Catholic section of the city the suckers still leave
those things in front of the stores in the open when they
make their deliveries. Too bad they don't leave a couple
of pounds of baloney too because we had to go buy that

at the all night deli for our morning sandwiches. We plan a big day (Brian and I) of going up to 168th St. to get ourselves a little codeine, enough medicine for a nice long Sunday afternoon nod.

After silly hash goofs with other loony heads, Brian and I split and taxi to 168th for the junk juice, but to no avail because the place we hit turns us down because the man's been bugging him about selling it to minors (you're supposed to be twenty-one to cop this stuff). After two more turnaways we almost give up hope when Brian decides to give a call to old Johnny Murry, who's been drinking six bottles a day since he was fifteen. "Try the real old guy on 163rd, he's cool and he's good for as many as you want; took a shopping bag's worth myself yesterday." Good old John. We hit 163rd and see the place he described right in the shadows of the ballroom where Malcolm X was gunned down not too long ago. We wait outside and discuss the fake names we're gonna use in the book you've got to sign when you buy this stuff. Brian goes in first and signs the book "James Bond" as he's paying his two dollars, then he exits and gives me the OK. I enter calmly, "One bottle of Robetussin, please . . ." but the old man behind the counter was already putting the stuff in the bag and getting out the book from the minute I walked in. He had the stuff right next to him on the shelf, in fact. I sign the book "Abe Lincoln," and give the guy two beans but he holds on to the bottle. I figured I blew it with my super fake John Jay, but instead he looks at me and says, "No good, I'm afraid Abe already got a bottle this morning," and he points out to me that some other medicine head already filled that one. "Oops," I say and erase it and scribble in "Wilt Chamberlain." He hands over the bag and I whistle out. We decide that two bottles is nicer than one so Brian enters again and signs it "George Washington." He's cool for another score. I go and write in "Al Swinburne" hoping there's no literary customers about and I get my second bottle. What a strange little old man. I really think that he thinks we're on the level. But at the rate he's going, he'll be retired soon just on medicine sales. There were six cats heading toward that store when we left and they all gave us the cute "I can dig it" face as they passed us and saw our little bags.

We caught a bus back down to Headquarters, got ten beers at the deli because they enhance the head with medicine, then picked a quiet corner in the living room and downed the syrup that was going to put us stacked right over the little day-to-day hassles of our post-puberty years. It has a thick taste and all, but you can bear it because you know what's coming after it. Actually, everyone else has split the apartment by now to dig a little touch tackle (except for the resident junkie, Jimmy Dantone, who's on the deep nod anyway) so we can enjoy ourselves in peace and quiet. Nothing worse than a loud mouth grass head when you're trying for a nice codeine head. We wait for the stuff to hit and Brian tells me about the little old man and woman down the block that have been drinking this stuff ever since they ran out of the old sex drive a few years back. Half an hour gone past now and Brian asks if it's hitting. "Just coming on," I tell him, and that was the last thing either of us muttered for seven hours when we both looked up to take a sip of beer and Brian says, "Do you feel it?" and I just mutter "Yeah, I feel it." What an understatement, I was so zonked that I'd let whole cigarettes burn down to the filter and burn my fingers without taking one drag. We had about six hours more of good solid nods and then sat around and rapped slowly about all our little visual dreams that passed in our heads clear as movies.

WINTER 65

I have this strange feeling that creeps up on me fairly often in classrooms, especially my first class in the morning, English. But this time it just happened in study hall up in the auditorium. It's just that I get this complete urge to suddenly take a machine gun and start firing like mad toward my right side. Not at anyone or anything unless they got in the way but that wouldn't matter much because I would aim fairly high. Just to do that a few seconds, like one whole round and that's it. I don't know why, dig, but I guess it would just release some tension or shit. Funny thing.

Then again on the same line whenever I'm on the toilet, ever since I was really young, I've got to have the door locked and, if I ain't reading or something, I usually fall into this thing that Germans are about to attack me and I have a pistol to protect me. I usually take a hairbrush or comb and hold it like it was a gun. Then I check about to see what *real* weapons I would have if it really happened, like the wooden stick on the plunger, the drainpipe (one of the best, real heavy metal . . . crack a skull in one shot), bottles, and shit like that but usually it's the gun thing. And when I'm done shitting, the fantasy's gone. I think a shrink would say it means something to do with sex. I just know I get the feeling a lot in class, and always in the john. It's a funny little game.

It makes you feel safe and ready for the Germans if they ever do bust in.

WINTER 65

My Marxist pal, Bunty, from my new school, finally talked me into going to one of his Communist Party meetings today. It was in this sleazy place on 11th St. called Webster Hall. All the girls looked like reformed Mary Magdalenes. Everyone moans a lot and plays folk songs, one of the requirements seems to be that you have to be ugly. I was wearing my seediest clothes and I still came off looking like Arnold Palmer or something. I dig these motherfuckers, but the speeches bored the shit out of me. I went home and told my old man how the government suppresses the proletariat from his due. "I am the proletariat, you dumb bastard," he said, "and I think those motherfuckers are off their rockers. Now get the hell inside and do your homework."

WINTER 65

I can't make out these private school dudes. Here they are with the richest parents around New York and I can't even lay down my pants in the locker room to take a shower without one of these cats rifling my pockets. Same bullshit with books; anyone that loses one seems to always take a loan on mine. I mean, man, I'm the poorest son of a bitch in this institution and I'm getting cleaned out. Just yesterday I got clipped for a five and last week some prick lifted me for a lid of dynamite grass I was about to deal. Today I got all evened out however. I hid down in the wrestling team locker room while my last study period was going on because I never go to that one anyway: it's only some lame senior who runs it and he ain't reporting me to no principals if he knows what's good for his ass. So here I am all of a sudden realizing that the team gets the privilege of early practice and in front of me are all these lockers minus their locks all chock full of goodies. I make the rounds after quietly shutting the door and getting fellow poor classmate David Lang to keep a lookout. I'm up to about fifteen beanos and checking out one of the last wallets left when David whispers from outside, "Get cool, it's Bluster." Shit, someone must have sent the word to Mr. Bluster, the principal, that I cut the study because he never comes to this part of the building unless he's checking for class cutters. I hear him outside reading a list to Lang with my name on it, asking if he's seen anyone. He says no and splits but I'm in one of the favorite hiding spots so I make a last minute move and squeeze into one of the floor lockers and shut the door behind me just barely fitting. I can hear Bluster checking through the door but he seems satisfied and moves on. I try to push the door of this tin trap open but, holy shit, you can't open the motherfucker from the inside! Instant panic of stuffy death with crusty jocks stuffed in my face. I can hardly move and I'm hoping Lang comes back but can't yell because Bluster might still be about. This hole in the wall stinks and I seem to have a javelin or something sticking right up against my balls. Best thing to do is stay calm, I figure, solutions will come. Now ten minutes and

no solution coming so I fuck it and start to yell. I hear
footsteps in the room. "In here, I'm in this locker here,"
I mutter and finally the door swings open. I fall out
gasping, a madras jock dangling off my nose. It's Ravi
Curry, Indian transfer student whose old man is a biggie
at the U.N., and star of the chess team. Ravi is a little
confused. I still got that wallet in my hand so I gotta be
quick to split. "Thanks Ravi, man, what those fucking
fraternities won't do before they let you in," I mumble
as I flip the jock to the cat and tip my ass back to study
hall. I got to go to the detention next weekend for missing that fucking class, but I came out fifteen dollars
richer even though my balls still hurt from whatever the
hell that thing in the locker was. I hope that Ravi won't
let any of those giant wrestlers know I was in that room
when they got looted because if he does I'm going to
kick his ass back to Bombay.

WINTER 65

We had a night game tonight up at Horace Mann and
Marc and I hung around after school and combed Central Park for some uppers. I found this fairly reliable,
guy who said he had some really strong ups and downs
and we copped ten of each . . . the ups for before the
game and the downs for after 'cause we were planning
to go to Headquarters afterwards for a Codeine medicine party and we'd have to come down from the speed
to get the most out of the Codeine, very complicated on
paper. So we're in the locker room before the game and
we take out the stash 'cause Anton Neutron and David

Lang had chipped in for them and wanted some too. I'd never seen this type of pills before, but I trusted that cat enough so I knew he wouldn't beat us, mainly because I know where he lives if he ever did screw us. Now here's twenty pills, capsules actually . . . ten red and black and ten a light pink. "Which ones did he say were the ups, Marc?" I casually ask. He gulps and says "I never asked, I thought you knew." This is very bad, as you must realize. So Lang butts in and says the red and blacks are ups but he didn't say it too assuredly.

"You know for sure?" I ask.

"No, but I think so," he answers.

"Well, I think the pinks are up," says Neutron.

"How come?"

" 'Cause I associate pink with lightness, and the others seem hard colored, like they might knock you out."

"He's got a point," chimes in Marc.

"Bullshit," I yell, "what kind of a lamebrain theory is that? Nembutols are light yellow, and they knock you on your ass."

"Maybe they're faded Seconals?"

"No, too light, this is their color, if they faded they'd be sticky."

"Bullshit."

"Fuck your mother, prick."

"All right! everybody cool it," I finally get to referee this thing.

We decided on a way to do it. We put one of each in Lang's bop hat, and Marc picked, the first one picked we'd take. He drew a black and red, we hesitated but took two each, got suited up and sat a minute; the rest of the team was already upstairs and Dudley Doolittle, our coach, sent the manager down to get us. We get

upstairs and get about three warmup shots in before the
giant horn honks and we gather around Doolittle for
last minute instructions, "You set up here and lay a pick
for him and if it's a man to man defense we use that
new 3-2 pattern we've been practicing, blah blah . . ."
Of course, all of this immediately boils down to my usual
individual game plan meaning, "If I get the fucking ball,
I'm shooting it, no matter if they play six thousand varieties of defense."

Then we're off, and for once against Horace Mann
we jump out in front and Anton Neutron and I are
hitting great on our shots and at the end of the first
quarter: our lead 23-16. Then the second quarter gets
whizzing and something strange begins to creep through
my body from head to little toe. I flash a peek at Marc,
Lang, and Neutron as a foul is called. Marc comes up
to me and mumbles in slow, low tone, "I got a feeling I
picked the wrong pill, you dig." I dug. No doubt about
it, we took the downest downers I may have ever downed.
My legs began to get the feeling someone slit a nice little
hole at the top of my thighs and poured in a few gallons
of liquid lead, I had a head on that felt like the rock of
Gibraltar . . . and Lang and Neutron just looked over
with ten pound eyeballs and nodded like, "You and your
fucking pick-from-the-hat trick." The guy shot the foul
and I went to jump for the rebound and I must have
risen all of half an inch off the ground. The other team's
dude who I normally leave looking at my shoelaces sailed
over me and easily laid it in. From there it got pathetic,
we scored three points in the whole quarter and were
literally staggering as the half ended with them winning
by eighteen points. Down in the lockers for the half time
talk Coach Doolittle, who wouldn't lose his cool if a tank

drove into his reading room, blew his cool. He turned nine shades of purple rage and told the four of us to get dressed, leave the building and report with him to the headmaster Monday morning. We did . . . got dressed as quick as our reflexes allowed and split and got a cab to my neighborhood to go up to Headquarters. It was a combination of everyone bitching how they were right and who was wrong, a pinch of foreseen disaster for Monday and intervals of total hysterical laughter about the whole farce. Finally there was a long silence as we got near Headquarters and Lang threw in the winner to break the ice, "I wish I was stoned, man, to forget about the whole shit." I just looked at him with Marc snoring, the prick had fallen completely out . . . "Lang," I shook my head, "you're a fucking jerkass, you dig, a real jerkass."

WINTER 65

If you never do anything to make yourself seen . . . like really seen, the type that makes people point, then you don't deserve to be seen at all. That's my theory, and not only on a basketball court, to look good while you're doing it is just as important as doing it good, and combine both and you've got it made. Presence is where it's at, but not the going out of your way to be noticed presence, but sneaky, shy presence (though it's all a part, you're still always aware). Presence like a cheetah rather than a chimp. They've both got it, but chimpy gotta jump his nuts around all day to get it, shy cheetah just sits in total nonchalance or moves a sec or two in his sexy strut.

Like it's easy on the court, you dunk a ball, dribble or pass behind the back . . . make a super layup out of an easy one (but not obvious you had to do it) then get fouled on it, say, and just walk to the line like you don't hear no "ohhs" and "ahhs," put on a "didn't you expect it" or "you dopey bastards" mug and walk lazily looking down all around like you were looking for the jock you faked off the dude who was guarding you. By the way, I don't know why the fuck I'm writing this shit . . . some dude asked me so I been thinking about it. Actually I ain't trying to sound like Helen Gurley Brown or shit, dig it, but if you see some dude acting like this one on court, and you can figure how to do it other ways you know where the dude is at. Fuck it anyway, I just couldn't think of anything else to write about anyway, no dope, no nooky, no queers following me today, I guess you start writing lame diaries like this.

SPRING 1965

SPRING 65

I made it to the subway today and I decided I'd skip school and go right on down to Times Square and wander around a little. I got off at 42nd and then hung out with the junkies in Horn & Hardart's for a while. They all shove donuts into coffee and shove it all into their mouths. I go over to the phone and call up the school and speak to the principal's secretary and tell her I'm puking all over my house and I got flies in my throat and all the lies I think I need as quick as I can so she don't hear the sound of the operator and know I'm not home. She seems to swallow the bullshit and I split to dig the streets. That's an advantage of going to a private school, like in public or Catholic school your parents have always got to be the ones who call, but in this place I can give them a little buzz every once in a while and be cool and everyone's happy. Actually I remember this jerk ass who went to some strict Catholic school that had a rule that if you were sick your old man had to call up to excuse you and we decided to cut out one nice day so he goes in the pizza place and calls the school and says, "Hello, this is my father, Ralphie Hornado ain't gonna be in today," and he hangs up and comes and tells me it's cool and I look at him and say, "You dumb prick."

So I buzz across 42nd to Grant's for a birchbeer and then just roam around for a good movie. I get to this empty part of 45th St. and near the side door of some theater is this great chick about thirty years old or so, but really foxy. She gives me the hook and I stroll over and see what's happening. She's heavy made-up and all but she doesn't come on like a hustler; she suggest she join me at the movies and then we go over to her place.

"I got grass, sweetie, you like grass." Sure I dig it, and we find a movie, of all things, *Born Free*. What nonsense, but this chick has led me up into thin air in the balcony and there isn't another person in the whole section. "This is why I picked this flick," she says, "privacy." And with that she lays her hand right across my cock and squeezes. I dig the balcony nooky so I sock my tongue into her mouth and get it on. Everything is humming nice when I reach on up her leg and work my way to her thing when, holy shit, I feel it and realize this freak HAS A COCK. I thought I would freak out on the spot so I jump up and make a mad dash down the stairs and take five about six blocks away from the crazy theater, still shaking. I walked back to the subway dazed but on the way I figure I'll play a few games in the penny arcade so I stop in and shoot a round at the shooting gallery. This one kid who looked like the Queens greaser type came over and says "You good?" I tell him I don't know, man what do you say to some shit like that. He says it again, "You good, man, that's all I want to know." Same answer. He asks if I want to bet on getting down eight moving rabbits in ten shots. I say "Make it $5," and the fish agrees. We put the money up with the spade attendant. I made ten. I take the dude's bread and split, saying, "I'm good." What a wise ass I am, but I wasn't too cool with that drag queen.

SPRING 65

Saw Bobby Blake today, a kleptomaniac, speed-freak friend, in the train on my way to school. He told me he was out on bail and had a trial coming up next week. I asked him what happened and (no lie) dig this: He got drunk Saturday night along with his usual super shot of speed and he's on his way home at three in the morning. On this quiet little street he decided to break into Gussie's Soda Fountain and check out the cash register. Tactlessly he threw the door of an old refrigerator that was lying around in the street through the glass door and climbed in over the glass still zonked as a doggie. Then he makes his way to the register but can't get the thing open, so he pushes it around some more to no avail. He gives up on it. As he's about to get his hot ass out of the place he looks up over the fountain, sees a sign of a giant ice cream soda and gets an incredible urge for that plus a grilled cheese sandwich. So he goes behind the counter and lights the stove, puts butter in the pan, makes a cheese sandwich, tosses it into the pan and the pan onto the fire. Then he goes about making an ice cream soda, using six flavors of ice cream. "I always wanted to use those syrup pumps and those professional ice cream scoopers and shoot in that seltzer the way old Gussie does," he told me. So he finishes making the soda, whip cream and all that, and he brings it around the counter and sits on a stool and starts into it. Then in come two cops, not believing for sure anything they see, Bobby not budging but biting away, cash register wrecked on the floor and the grilled cheese sandwich which Bobby forgot about burning to a crisp. "He must be on one of those hell infested drugs." "S.D.S. my ass, you dumb harp," Bobby said, and he rapped the cop for ten minutes about how he worked there and just happened to be passing when he saw what happened and was wishing for an ice cream soda besides. "They

took me away," he told me, "with my grilled cheese still
burning, the dumb bastards."

SPRING 65

I'm lying on the sofa digging SUPERMAN on TV after
dinner and my moms is sorting through the mail of the
day: *Life*, a letter from the Bartender's Union, *The Catholic News* (why they insist on sending that rag here I have
no idea. We never pay the little frog that comes around
to collect for it. I think anyone with an Irish name they
send it to on a hunch), a bill from Macy's and, as my
old lady makes me quick to know, a letter from my
principal, Mr. Bluster. She opens it like a savage . . . a
short note: "Jim has become a constant enigma around
here as you might well detect from the report you received last week. Please attend parents' day next week
(date . . . blah blah, cocktails served) as Jim's teachers
and I are anxious to see you about this."

She beams in on me in a manner rather mean, "What
happened to this report card crap last week?"

"Well, dig, I heard a lot didn't get out, some mail
hassles . . . Eggie called me last night and mentioned he
didn't get one either."

Of course that's jive, I simply knew what day it was
coming and skipped practice, intercepted it, dug what
an atrocity it was and now it's a bed of shreds at the
bottom of the dumbwaiter shaft. "What the hell does
enigma mean?" she asks my brother. He shrugs, a bagful
of potato chips in his mouth. I grab the big book and
blurt out in dictionary language, "Enigma: a model

of perfection, an example used to have others strive toward. E.g., He was a constant enigma among his math classmates." I calmly fold the big volume and bury it back into the shelves, my brother rolling around the floor choking on potato chips. My old lady heads over to the bookcase . . . this diary fades out with bad ending.

SPRING 65

Saw Bobby Blake again tonight, remember him, robbed Gussie's last week and got busted eating an ice cream soda? that's the guy. Well tonight we were heading up to Headquarters really late, about four in the morning, and hear a huge crash of glass at the end of the block. We run down to check it out (I'm on a light pill head and hope it ain't no fight 'cause that's one scene I will definitely be unable to handle). We get to Jack's Clothing Shop and see a small gang of bar rats hanging around in front of the smashed front window, and inside is Bobby, standing there taking pants off the display dummies and handing them out to the eager crowd. Straight looking little old men were wandering by, in fact, and they seemed to treat the whole thing casually as hell and take a nice pair of pants, tip their little brims and shuffle off like this happened every night. Bobby of course was rapping a storm, doing some kind of auction type bit. He was plainly wrecked on speed. "Step right up, you drunken bastards, be you hippie or junkie, have a free pair on me." I forgot to mention he usually lapses into rhymes when he really gets whacked out. Just about this point, the cops were tooling in full force, and the crowd took to the wind in several directions. Bobby, in his usual manner, stood his ground and offered the man a free pair of work pants as they dragged him off to the station.

SPRING 65

There is a rule at the private school I go to that no students are allowed to leave the building until school is out for the day because too many saps have been taken off or beat up around here. One of my teachers in fact just the other day got mugged walking down Columbus on his way home. But David Lang, and Marc, and Anton Neutron and I always check out after lunch to kill time. Sometimes in fact we get high. Today Lang and I hopped out the lunch room window and went down to 89th to cop some H. Risky copping hard dope there, lots of beat artists, but two P.R.s, Lefty and Popo, are trustworthy enough and Popo just happens to be there. We get two each. "Dynamite," says Popo, a word which is muttered by every dealer in the city no matter what the fuck they're dishing out to you. Our original plan is to sniff the shit in math class but some creep with a spike says he'll let us get off with him in the basement down the street if we both lay a taste on him. OK with us we tell him but it better be quick, we got ten minutes to get back. We pop into the cellar, whip off my belt and tie up, throw the four bags in the cooker and I draw up my count first, shoot some back in the cooker for the mooch and get a quick hit, boot it three times and almost land on my ass with an o.d. "This stuff is not bullshit, Lang you better be cool." He gets off with his usual bad touch, takes about ten holes in his arm before he hits a main and feels it so much right off that he don't even boot the shit. This cellar scent ain't too cool with me so we don't stick around for shooting any breeze and leave the other cat there by himself and stumble out onto 89th where a cop car stops and pulls us over. We got our school blazers on so he asks us what we're doing coming out of that basement and I tell him, glassy-eyed and pulling up my pants which are now falling down because I realize I left my belt down with that cat who didn't get off yet, tell the man that we are on a social work project and are taking a survey in that building. They swallow, we split. Back to the school in through the gym door and up to math class on total nod, nobody any the wiser except Marc and Neutron who are pissed off that we didn't bring them along.

SPRING 65

A little girl, about ten years old, came over to me today in some far out Bronx redneck neighborhood and asked me why my hair was so long and I told her because I like it that way. She answers, "I'll bet you're against the war, huh?" "Yep," I told her.

"Well, do you believe in God?"

"Don't really think about it the same way as you," I say.

"Don't you think that Christ was God?"

"Do you?"

"Yes," she says quick.

"Do you think that Christ would fight in the war?"

She replied, "Yep."

"Well, did you ever read about Christ killing, or using a gun?"

"No."

"Well, do you think he would fight in the war?"

"I guess not," she finally said, and walked right on.

"Then tell that to your nun and your friends," I shouted. She sort of smiled.

I realize this was all a wee trite, but what a cute little girl, you should have seen her. Maybe she'll even drop out of her sixth grade class Monday. She was a minor genius with adorable freckles.

SUMMER 1965

SUMMER 65

Some old Navy friends of Brian's, two seeds from the sticks in Omaha, are visiting N.Y. for the first time and shacking up in Headquarters, a place they constantly refuse to believe is really happening. Like the dudes are good people but a bit naïve . . . minute they got off the bus at Port Authority some junkie con and his partner did a fast take on one of them in the bathroom, like as he put it, "I finished talking to this here fellah, you see, when I look down and see mah bag is gone, plumb amiss, so was the fellah's friends, in fact, who the fellah told me had a singing engagement at this Plaza Room in a hotel by the same name and had to take off. Don't know for the life what coulda gone done to my satch, nice fellah warned me you gotta watch yourself each minute in this town or you had it. Then he took off too, said he was their piano player . . . told me I could drop down to see them with some friends any night, any you fellahs know this Plaza place? Any good?" "Oh my lord," I mumble and sink back into a nod in the corner . . . slowly. Then they smoked some grass (Brian already had turned them on in the Navy) and they hassled forty-five minutes trying to get down subway directions to the Statue of Liberty, musta asked the same fucking questions eight times each and all they had to do was take the "E" right down the street to the last stop, not even a switch. The whole place was in tears over the cats. Personally they just bothered my nod, so finally I got up and took them myself . . . I ain't never been to the Statue of Liberty anyway, nor the Empire State Building.

SUMMER 65

The fag hustling scene gets hairier and hairier all the time. I mean what happened to the old fashioned homo who just wanted to take you home and suck your dick? They're getting more and more like those seals up in Alaska I signed a petition for at school the other day, a species going down at an incredible rate. You just don't know what the next trick you pick up is gonna whip out of his attaché case these days . . . Handcuffs, masks, snakes (yeah, that's right, real ones), chains, whips, last week a guy had a pet parrot that he had eat grapes out of my pubic hair. (He had a leather "muff" for my cock to insure me against any danger of the dumb bird getting smart and snatching off my main asset). It's all out of hand as far as I'm concerned, I'm taking a vacation for a few weeks before I go zoo . . . I'd rather go back to ripping off old ladies or something sensible.

I just want to run down a few cases on paper before I develop heavy guilt feelings.

Let's start with Dave . . . not the strangest of the last two weeks but a man with a definite problem. He picks me up on the "meat rack" on Third Avenue and does he want to suck dick? No way. Dave is a fifty-five-year-old well off V.P. of a popular yogurt company and he's got an executive box at Yankee Stadium . . . and Dave is going to pay me fifty bills if I attend the day's double header with him. This *really* happened . . . I bullshit you not . . . I am sane, it takes a little dope now and then . . . but I have maintained sanity. Every little leaguer in N.Y. is on his old man to get good seats for a ball game and I'm getting paid for it . . . besides the extra satisfaction for me of sitting there watching and remembering the years I slave labored around that joint selling popcorn in 90 degrees and cold drinks at 33 degrees; I felt great having old Dave buying me beers from all those old-time hawkers there who used to call me a lazy bastard and give me shit . . . I even saw my old foreman who fired me and gave him a nice big gesture in front of his crew. But to tell you the truth I'm no big baseball fan and staying to the last out of a whole double header was one of the most boring scenes that ever went down. Dave was a fanatic, really laying on the old "fan" bullshit . . . I had to fake it along for the four and a half hours just like I got to fake it in bed . . . but I'd rather get a boring blow job for half an hour any time instead of this crap, in fact I tapped the price up to seventy-five before the second game began, because "It was taking up precious time and money." Dave forked over an even hundred. It didn't really surprise me . . . how can anything surprise you in the middle of a scene like that? I have no idea what the fruit's motive was in all this . . . he did give me a squeeze on the thigh whenever a Yankee got a hit but that was as far as it went. I guess he was just another lonely man . . . but why the bread? When he let me out of the cab at the "Rack" I gave the souvenir Yankee cap he bought me to this drag queen on the scene there who's got the hots for Mickey Mantle "in those tight pin-stripe pants he wears on the field."

A few days before my day at the ball park some CPA gets me up to his hotel room and leads me into the bathroom. He's got a cat tied to the seat of the toilet and a bubble bath all set for someone to jump in. I excused myself for a second and went over to the kitchenette and popped a couple of Valiums . . . I was already loaded on junk but I could see this was going to be strictly

from fruit. When I got back in the john he was already
naked and in the tub frosted in bubbles . . . the poor cat
was still chained to the john seat, yelping away. The guy
laid his plan on me. He wants me to whip the cat dead
after I first piss on him in his bubble bath, then when
the cat has had it I'm to jerk off into his mouth while
he's still in the tub. Out from under the bubbles he hands
me a whip, a tiny cat size whip with leather fringes laced
with broken ends of razors. I did not like this man. I
didn't like him at all, and too bad for him I was very
stoned and in a cat-loving mood so I decided to express
my dislike. I untied the cat, he tried to get up and stop
me, I punched his chump face, he landed back on his
ass in the tub and I gave him the whip across the chest . . .
a nasty wound. He was a little dazed now . . . I grabbed
his hair, opened his mouth and pissed in it . . . he spit
it out, the piss mixing with the blood oozing from his
lip from the punch and he let out a slow motion yell at
the sting of urine dripping into the cuts on his chest.
He sank under water to cool the burn, I rifled his wallet
for sixty bucks, picked up the kitty and split.

SUMMER 65

I'm riding uptown on the "A" train tonight, half on the
nod and half trying to read a sports magazine. There's
this chick that gets on at 175th St., a real secretary-
stewardess type with big tits and the beehive hair job.
She's right across the way from me, hardly any people
in the car, and here she is tossing this spread toward me

so wide I can see her powder blue panties. What do these faces want out of me, an athletic youth trying to enjoy a nice heroin head and harmless magazine? Finally I got up and went over to her and asked her if she could please close her legs, I'm barely fifteen years old and it's distracting and, frankly, lewd. Then I went over and sat down again.

SUMMER 65

Deborah Duckster, the debutante, Ned the fag, Marc Clutcher, and I were up bullshitting the night at pal Joey's apartment on East 10th Street. By about five a.m. we were all whacked out from too much dope and too many late show TV ads about buying lots for cheap in some New Jersey swamp etc. that we decide to screw the ride uptown and shack up there for the night. First we plan to make it to RATNER'S for some mushroom soup breakfast. We walk out into pleasant morning air and what horrible bringdown is there to greet us: out on the sidewalk in front of the next building a totally naked woman groaning in slow pain, blood splashed all over the pavement. Before I know it, in some strange dope flash I'm next to her, and her hand reaches into mine holding tight she mumbles, "I let them . . ." She must have been about twenty-five and a pretty face under the red and tangled hair all knotted by blood. I can't do anything but hold her hand and look around at everyone else. I spot a long deep gorge in her ankle and it's oozing blood in slowmotion spurts. Deborah half-faints onto a car hood. Joey's hopping steps to call an ambulance and the cops. Ned the fag is zonked on repulsion. She keeps mumbling groan talk; my first thought was she was some junkie hooker from up Third Avenue who crossed a pimp and got hacked up in a car and dumped here. But she's too tan and pretty to be a junkie-whore, I could see the outline of white skin from the strap marks of a bikini. Third Ave. and Fourteenth St. hookers are the cheapest and ugliest around and they sure don't spend their days at beaches getting tans. Then I spot Ned the fag staring horribly up the building's façade and I realized the obvious. The fifth floor window was open to the hilt: this chick had taken a dry dive. Joey nodded as I looked at the window . . . I was the last one to figure it out. And she's still clutching me and I keep letting soft gestures out . . . What the fuck am I supposed to say? Stoned from such strong grass we smoked, here in the cosmos holding a suicide case at five a.m.? Now a bunch of morning people surround us and finally a cop car pulls up . . . I walk over and bum a smoke from a dog walker, my hand shaking badly. The cops toss a blanket over her body and a few questions at us. They want to know why Deborah and Ned keep fainting on each other if we don't know who she is. I explain we're not used to walking out to a dry dive case so early in the morning, dumb ass cops. I float back into Joey's apartment with that pleading face of hers (for who? for what?) on my mind, took a bang of H and went off to nod, my nerves calmed a bit . . . it will all come back. These things happen.

SUMMER 65

If there were, say, a book like "The Pervert's Guide To New York City," the bathroom at Grand Central Terminal should, without any doubts, figure in it. The bathrooms in the subways themselves are bad enough, but at least you've got the Transit fuzz popping in and out of them often enough so the pervies are uptight to directly take a grab at you, but not so at old Grand Central, where anything might go. I was catching a train up to Rye, N.Y. tonight to visit old neighborhood chum Willie at, I'd say, just after five-thirty p.m. Man, all those business cats just lined up along the piss machines (there must be forty machines, whatever the hell you call them, that's right, urinals, lined next to each other) and then along with them the usual seedy dudes, hustlers, etc. and all these eyes peeking down at the guy next to me who's peeking down at me along with the guy on my other side and jacking off like madmen, forty arms like pistons pumping back and forth at incredible rates. Not a bit of class in the entire place, just a bunch of office worker closet queens getting off their rocks before they miss the 5:50. Any of those Westchester housewives that ain't had too much lately can come down here and find out why. But the peeky-boo scene is old hat and that goes on in any john, it's just that here you suddenly feel a hand moving across your leg and grabbing your fucking cock. No raised eyebrows about it from anyone, fuck, I'm beginning to think I'm the only person in the place that came down just for normal body functions. I jumped back in the middle of pissing while this stately chap grabbed me and I wound up spraying all over the Brooks Brothers number the guy is wearing. I had to move

down to another whatever they are to finish it off. Same
bit. This cat next to me now I thought for a second was
going to pull out a pair of binoculars. It's true, guys even
sucking dick down there right in front of other cases if
the "attendant" isn't looking. Shit, what am I gonna do,
complain to this "attendant" about what's happening.
He looks like he might pull my jeans down and bugger
me on the spot. Besides, rarely these days do I complain
about anything.

The businessmen are the worst, no doubt. And they
all have a thing about checking out the young guys. I've
seen cats who are probably vice-presidents of toothpaste
firms or shit fighting over the piss machine next to me.
This form of flattery will get them nowhere with me.
Spades too, they dig getting next to the spades and tuning in on a little black stuff. Don't ever let your kiddie
go pee-pee in that joint by himself, and if you do and
he comes back up the stairs smiling, I suggest you have
a little chat with the boy.

SUMMER 65

I'm going back a bit in this diary today because this
strange episode's been hitting me on and off most of
the day. Crumb day, I might add, the really boring type
rain . . . I was about nine. My friend Kenny and I would
spend a lot of time hanging around the cellar of our
apartment house, mostly tossing a ball back and forth
or listening to the radio. The superintendent of the place,
Buddy, was a jolly dude who was the laziest bastard on

earth but who, when bugged enough, would and could fix anything any tenant had a bitch over. He's an on and off drunk who is totally on lately, so his job seems hanging on pretty thin wire. He digs us though, and let us hang around like the older cats who would play big card games in the boiler room. It was a seedy and dark, smelly place now that I think about it. I guess that's why I dug it. I know these other guys, in fact, that hung around in an old busted down news truck for about two years without once realizing what a boring idea it was.

This particular day in mind something really strange happened. Kenny and I were flopping around as usual, watching the card game when one of the older guys' younger sisters, Sharron, who was about thirteen and a little funny looking with a lot of make-up, and her friend Lou-Lou, dropped in. After Kevin and I moved into the bigger room, they followed us, watching us play baby baseball for awhile and suggested that we go into the radio room and check it out. We got in there and they immediately suggest that we play a little game that was unfamiliar to both Kenny and me, "Doctor." We said great, how's it go? "Well," Lou-Lou piped in, "the game is, in this case, 'Nurses' . . . Now you and Kenny take off your pants and Sharron and I give you an examination." Total mystery to both of us but we follow nurse's orders and drop our little jeans. Kevin peeked over at me and I peeked over at him and realizing our young pricks were more or less the same size we gave cool smiles. The two girls gave cool smiles too, in fact, they immediately whipped off their dresses to even things out, and they literally did "even things out" 'cause I knew girls were different than boys in that sense and that's what was baffling. You see it was my first exposure to drag queens and I noticed to my complete surprise that they had little pee-pees too.

SUMMER 65

We got off in the park tonight with some nice scag that Joey L. copped down around Chelsea and we hit into the BUCKET OF BLOOD, that friendly neighborhood tavern, totally twisted. Jimmy Mancole and Henry rapped to Joey at the bar. Brian and I sat in the booth on the nod. Everything was cool until three gentlemen strutted in through the side door and headed toward the bar. They were all wearing trench coats and little feathered fedoras, two white guys and one black. They had a slightly-for-the-worse grey car parked in front. Their outfits meant one of two things: they were either basketball scouts or narcotics cops. Since basketball scouts seldom hung around in the BUCKET, it seemed likely they were the latter. In fact it couldn't have been more obvious if all three had little red lights spinning around the tops of their fedoras. Brian straightened up from his nod when I poked him but he just took one look at them, mumbled "Corny ass bastards, huh?" and went right back down into the dream machine. The narcs just sat around at the bar and talked among themselves, satisfied that they were getting everyone uptight. Finally big Mike McIntosh broke the silence by saying out loud, "Why don't those fucking cops get the fuck out of here?"

"What did you say?" the spade cop asked.

"I said get the fuck out."

The narcs moved over to Mike, a not too bright pot-acid (I turned him on to it for the first and last time last week, he kept thinking he was in a firehouse that he couldn't get out of) head, a former speed freak and a junkie . . . Occupation: dig it, a fucking LONGSHORE-MAN. I called aside Baby Joey, "Tell these guys to cool it, I'm dirty and these guys are gonna start checking." "YOU'RE dirty," he told me, "Shit, I got half a bundle on me, that's a pushing rap, three years on the Rocke-feller program." (The Rockefeller program is nothing more than a jail for junkies upstate, like you break "rocks next to the other fellow," so to speak.) So the black cop is standing up to Mike and told him to step out. "Not while you're carrying that fucking toy under your jacket," Mike told him. The Spade laid his gun on the other cop. This was incredible, it was like the old West or some-thing. I slipped into the bathroom and hid my bags under the toilet pipes. By this time all the junkies had ordered beers instead of the Cokes in front of them because a narc notices something a little suspicious when he walks into a bar and everyone is nursing a Coke. "Mike will kick the bastard's ass in." Brian popped up from his nod to whisper, and he probably would have too but he'd also be down in the old precinct five minutes after. Eventually the white narc stepped in and cooled it: "Now this man is an officer of the N.Y.C. Police De-partment, son, and he has the power to arrest you if you so much as raise one fist to him." The bartender pulled Mike aside and translated this. Peter walked Mike out of the bar and down the street to cool him. The narcs stayed a few minutes longer and started to leave, giving all of us a double take and one of them, I think it was the black one, says, "This place is hot, we know what goes on, and I'm warning you the whole bunch of you are going to get burned soon." Brian looked up again, "Corny fucks, I told you they were." The car pulled out and we all looked at the beers in disgust and pushed them aside and ordered more Cokes.

SUMMER 65

It's always been the same, growing up in Manhattan, especially when I was a little younger, the idea of living within a giant archer's target . . . for use by the bad Russia bowman with the atomic arrows. Today I was hustling around Times Sq. and thought about it and got a strange rush of unknown sex giddiness off the idea of leaning here and now against a wall in leather pants throwing pouting eyes at customers strolling by dead in the center of the target . . . ground zero in one big fireball Island. I thought of the explosion's eye as one giant plutonium red cunt that would suck me up and in and just totally devour and melt me into its raw wet walls of white heat in pure orgasm. And then again, aside from fantasy like this that springs up from constant drills in schools and TV flashes, a hideous fear which I barely feel now. After all these years of worry and nightmares over it (I remember my brother enticing me on to panic during the Cuban crisis saying they were coming any minute) I think by now I'd feel very left out if they dropped the bomb and it didn't get me.

SUMMER 65

Fucked up yesterday, lost our last game in the summer 15-and-under league up at George Washington High School, and that deuced us out of the championship game today. We had a good squad, mostly cats from down the block in the projects but they had a rule that no Varsity players could play. That ruined our chances of using big Lewie Alcindor even though he's from the neighborhood and all. I mean, shit, most of the teams got ringers but it's a little difficult to sneak in a seven foot All-Everything cat onto a court. He can't exactly use a fucking pair of sunglasses, dig? So I go up to watch the game today and pick up my trophy for the all-league team and what a hassle is steaming as I bop into the gym. THE SUGAR BOWL ALL-STARS, one of the teams playing, are in a rage bitching about the ringers on RUTGERS team. So true! those cats didn't have a dude under eighteen running for them, none of them played school ball, but they were some of the best playground players in Harlem. I walked over and was rapping to a few friends, Vaughn Harper, an All-American from Boys High, and Earl Manigault, a Harlem legend of 5 ft. 10 in. who can take a half dollar off the top of a backboard. He's invariably on and off his school team because of drug scenes and other shit. These two cats are, with big Lew, the best high school players in the city. Finally the captain of SUGAR BOWL points over to us and tells the other team and the man who runs the gig that if they're gonna use that team, that their team's gonna use Harper, "Goat" Manigault, and me. The bossman axes the idea of letting in Harper and "Goat" but says they can use me, which is fine with the

other team who don't even know who the fuck this white
boy is. Before I say a fucking word I get a uniform tossed
in my mug and since there're bunches of chicks in the
stands, my new team mates are huddling around me
and I whip on the shit and start warming up. Big fucking
difference I'm gonna make 'cause we need leapers for
the boards and no backcourt dude like me. Anyway the
slaughter starts and I'm hitting long jumpers like a fucker
(I gotta say that I always burn up that gym, something
about it that I just can't miss, crazy) so we're holding
our own by the half and I got twenty-eight points, each
move of which I make sticks out like a hardon because
I'm the only whiteman on the court and looking around,
in the entire fucking place, in fact; my bright blond-red
hair making me the whitest whitey this league has ever
seen. So in short we made a good show for a team our
age, but can't keep up with the other dudes and lose by
ten, but that ain't bad and I got myself forty-seven points
and at least got to play for once with these cats I've always
had to play against in various tournaments since Biddy
League days. Then to bust all kinds of balls, the bossman
gets some college scout in the stands to testify the other
team got at least three ringers he knows and we are
awarded the champ bit. After the gold is handed out
and all (I didn't get a trophy for the game 'cause they
were one short and I had to say "fuck it," but got an
outofsight plaque for All-League), we go in a corner and
pose a team picture for the Harlem paper, "The Amsterdam News." We're waiting for the birdie to click
when the photog calls over the SUGAR BOWL coach
and whispers something to him who then walks over to
me and mumbles, "Dig, my man, don't know how to say
this but for, well, . . ." I cut him short and told him I

got the message and stepped out of the pix. I guess I would have messed up the texture of the shot or something. Or maybe they didn't want to let the readers get to see that the high scorer was a fucking white boy.

SUMMER 65

Brian, Barry, Butch and I were smoking grass up in the woods of Inwood Park and after awhile we all caught the incredible grass hunger and decided to make it down to 207th St. for some "belly bombs" at the hamburger joint there. On the way we met a few more heads, also stoned, and began to realize as we got closer to the dive that no one had enough bread for a fucking pretzel stick. We had to think this over. Being stoned, we all agreed that hunger demands food, money or not, and that only people who were not hungry should pay for the food because it is in that instance more a luxury than necessity. This theory seems a little obscure now, but at the time it made profound sense. We then mapped out a way to pull it off. This place just opened last week and the guys who work there are pure cretins, so Barry and I figured we could handle it and told the rest of them to wait back in the park. We go in and order twenty-seven burgers with the works to go. "Got a hungry poker crowd upstairs," I say to the jerk who's flopping burgers. The guy says, "Yeah, nothing like a bite after a few hours of cards." The sap. "Any drinks?" he adds. Barry tells him nine Cokes. So everything is all set with burgers and sodas in separate bags and the guy's figuring it out on a paper hat. Meanwhile Barry takes the burgers and says, "You got enough to cover it, right Jim?" "Sure, I'll handle it," I say and he starts out the door and slowly creeps up the block. Then the guy looks up and mumbles some ridiculous price and I reach back for my wallet and say suddenly, "Oh, Jesus, I just remembered, one coffee for my old lady." The guy spins and pulls the coffee knob and off I go, running my balls off with Barry half way up the block, down into Cal, the dope-dealing superintendent's, cellar, and over a fence into an alley leading us right near the church, with a clear path down to the park.

SUMMER 65

I'm sick of the city heat and all its bullshit so I throw my sneakers and a bathing suit into my little airlines bag and take the train down to Grand Central to catch the rush hour express for Rye, N.Y. to visit old friend Willie Goodbody who moved up there a year ago and has a nice scene going for himself. I can't resist hitting the drug store in the station for a bottle of Codeine cough syrup to make the train ride more peaceful and I get a bottle and a can of beer at the deli with my fake draft card and go downstairs to the men's room to slug it down. As usual, at this time (five p.m.), the place is packed with all the executive fairies peeking at each other's thing and pulling off all along the long row of those piss machines; I pass that by and put a dime in the turnstile and pick out a toilet stall where I can drink up in private. So I'm sitting on the seat in one slugging down the horrible tasting stuff and god damn it, this fairy's head is looking up from under the barrier of the next stall and he's there reaching his hand out at my cock! I let fly a clean kick right into the queen's mug and I think he got the message. Shit, if a cop came along, I'd be in a lot more trouble than him if he saw I was doing medicine. I finished up quick, can't get away from them fags anywhere these days. So I get on the Rye train just in time and get a seat. It's a fairly quick ride; this is the express so we don't gotta stop at all them cracker towns on the way, just about three stops and, as the song goes, "I'll be there," clean air and cool water. By the first stop the Codeine is hitting and, good lord, I feel loose. Of course since I've been fucking with junk too much lately the head ain't that heavy, but it's better than I expected. Then we pull into Mt. Vernon and I figure it would be nice to do up one of the reefers I brought along, so I sneak calmly into the john and do one up real quick. The shit is *smoking*. I get paranoid about walking back to my seat without cracking up looking at all them executive creeps in uniform with their little fedoras and them dumb little cases they carry that usually got nothing but a pencil in them every time I see a dude open one. Finally I figure I gotta make my move and the minute I open the door I could swear that everyone in the car turns right around and simultaneously focused their eyes right on me like they all had x-ray vision and could see what I was doing the whole time I was in the john. The paranoia was so heavy I thought they were all gonna heave me off under the tracks or shit. It seemed an hour walking down that aisle back to my seat and then I just huddled there, pretending I was reading but secretly scared shit and goofing on all them at the same time. I ain't doing that again unless there's some fellow freaks on board.

_____ SUMMER 65

It seems I've picked up the clap over the weekend from some debutante little beaver in "posh" Rye, N.Y. Never know where the fuck it's gonna get yer. Anyway it's quite a bringdown waking up with your underwear a mass of red-brown blotches, all stiff as cardboard except where the gooey fresh blobs are. I got up and pissed. It felt like I was shooting boiling water out of me. I noticed when I changed my undies that the drip was changing color on me now. It was becoming a puss green. Call Tony: "Don't go to the Board of Health whatever you do. They won't let you out without finding out the name of every girl you ever touched, then they send out these notices to all your chicks, next thing you know you can't get a girl to talk to you." He gives me the address of a cool doctor on the fringe of Harlem who handles all the junkies and whores there and will report nothing, eight bucks. I have a wake-up shot of dope and hop downtown on the train. I've been trying to just sniff my dope lately but it ain't working as usual. So I get in this office and it's as seedy as Tony made out. Every case of social disease in the city is in this dump. Cute tiny nurse asks me the trouble. That threw me a bit. I just sorta made some rubbery face and nodded down and pointed at my crotch. She asks if I have a discharge. I dumbly thought she meant from the Army so I say "no" but then she told

me she means from my penis and I blush, nod "yes,"
and cop a quick seat. Few minutes and this hulk of a
doctor calls my name and asks me to step in. I get in
the office, tell him I got a "discharge" and he don't even
look, just has me pull down my pants and rams two big
hypos in my ass, hands me three pills to take and puts
out the palm for the bread. I ask if he ain't even gonna
look at the thing but he tells me it's 90% I got the clap
and he hates looking at the disgusting shit anyway. What
a quack or what a genius this mug is, but whatever he
is he made me feel a lack of security going home. But
it's been eight hours now and the hideous green slime
has ceased to spout any further so I assume all is back
in order, so to speak.

SUMMER 65

I'm gonna be fifteen soon and the summer's "Pepsi-
Cola" heroin habit is tightening more and more around
me. I'm getting that feeling for the first time since I lost
my virgin veins at thirteen that I gotta start getting my
ass together 'cause school's coming at me mighty quick
and no way of doing that scene with a habit. A "Pepsi-
Cola" is a small habit, a first habit that finally sneaks up
on you while you're telling yourself, "Shit, I been fucking
around with junk for three years and I know when to
lay off and I ain't getting me no habit." But one morning
you wake up, suddenly your nose is running and your
eyes are tearing and the leg and back muscles start feeling tight and heavy. The laugh's on you finally, no matter how long you think you got it "under control." So

now I look in the mirror and realize I better cut loose, no jiving myself any longer.

Shit it ain't easy. I've been on stuff almost everyday the last three months or so, and add that to the "off and on" tricks for these past three years. I got leg pains like I just played six ballgames on top of each other, eyes heavy and wet. But the worst part of all: that tiny voice reaching over your neck, feeding you all them anxieties, "First just one last one, you can start quitting tomorrow." Shit like that every second, you can't shake it loose. You see a spoon and all you think of is cooking up stuff on it, my arms and hands filled with tracks and I just gotta sit in chumpy Headquarters here, no one here for once in a blue moon, because one step outside and the pool-room's like a magnet filled with dealers. And what about when Mancole or some other user gets back here and gets off in front of me? Can't even imagine what changes that's gonna hand me. I best get out to the country or shit, never gonna make it here . . . getting too nervous to even write about it. No use taking downers though, that just delays it, I got to do something to off that little voice, I can gladly take sore muscles but my mind can't handle the monkey back there. And I used to laugh at the corny monkey phrase too, I had it under "control" all the way to sitting and sneezing a lot on this fucking lice sofa wanting to scream my balls off.

FALL 1965

FALL 1965

It's been about two weeks now being back in school and I got the word from this senior that the best chicks on the private school scene go to The Professional Children's School down on 60th St. I know a chick from my neighborhood, Deborah Duckster, who's an out of sight looking model who goes there and I've been hanging out in the "Blimpies" sandwich shop on 56th St. with that scene and going out with this Italian actress chick who is thirteen but looks about twenty-five. It's weird 'cause everyone is either a model or actress or ballet dancer and they're fanatic about their work and each new person I meet is always asking me what I do. What the fuck do I do? I was the baby in the Johnson & Johnson baby powder ad when I was six months old but I ain't about to let that shit out. I'm cool, that's all, you motherfuckers. The guys are worst . . . on super ego trips, mostly swishy dudes too. This one cat who's an actor is marbles. Today he charged into "Blimpies," knocking people over with this mad look on his mug, holding up a letter screaming, "I got it, I got the lead!" Big shit for the fruit. Type of guy you expect every time you pass a lamp post for him to swing up on it and break out into some Gene Kelly number. The ballerinas are maniacs. They all have the same walk. I can spot one anywhere now. I went out with this dancer one night and she had just found out this nut was giving a speech on "The Great Gap: connections between ballet and modern dance." So she drags me there instead of the movie I was up for. The Great Gap was the great crap . . . I took a downer and a nod. I get her home, no one there, and she invites me in and she was strictly no touchy and kissed like a cow, never saw her since because she practices twenty hours a day and to boot she writes me letters saying she misses me like I was in China. They got no friends 'cause they've been run around by mommy since they were two with those fucking portfolios they all carry. But they got a few cats who don't do nothing special but somehow go there anyway and I can dig them, and I guess it's my ego thing to want to bullshit about my chick being on TV and all like this one I dig now, and for each prude in the place there's a slut to match, and often rich sluts, and every young man needs a rich slut.

FALL 65

When they dropped them A-bombs on Japsville I wasn't even an idea, but I paid for it anyhow all through growing up and I'm still paying. The "war baby" gig ain't no smartass headshrinker's dumb theory, and all the people who grew up when I did can tell you that. I used to have horrible dreams of goblins in tiny planes circling my room and bombing my bed most every night age six or seven; every time a fire truck or an ambulance passed the house I was pissing with fear in my mother's arms with the idea that it was the air raid finally come, and *real* air raid drills *still* freak me when I'm stoned. The worst is the old buggers can't believe it's real, that it could ever happen to us. Now there's a big peace move growing in this country and my old man and the rest are calling me a creep and saying it's all some commie who brainwashed us all, it's them fucking commies, that's all. Shit I don't give a royal screw what a commie is. It's just the dreams we remember that make us want to end your nuclear games. I think more about a fire truck passing late at night than I do about Karl Marx when I'm out yelling for them to fuck your wars, I don't pay no dues to no commies, that's some dream dreamed up to take the rap for you. The Russians are drags too, you're all old men drags, scheming governments of death and blinding white hair.

FALL 65

Headquarters is in its usual end of the month condition of wet floors from spilt beer and flaked with bottles, cans, cigarette butts, etc. covering the deck inch to inch. Not to mention dirty socks and underwear, ripped up and come-upon playmates of the month and all the other junk shit items. You see, once a month there's one huge cleanup usually by some chicks we gather up and for the first week it's fair, the second week "careless" and the next two a total mess, a three-room ashtray. We're all used to it though. Messy house don't matter, dirt don't matter (if it does we might as well all stop breathing). Keeping your head in order is what counts, tidiness never saved anyone the good times we have, and all that means freedom. Like to sit in this awful mess and maybe smoke some dope and watch some innocuous shit on a dumb glass tube and feel fine about it and know there's really nothing you have to do, ever, but feel your warm friend's silent content is what this place is about. You don't feel guilty about not fighting a war or carrying signs to protest it either. We've just mastered the life of doing nothing, which when you think about it, may be the hardest thing of all to do.

FALL 65

The narco cops are the most full of shit motherfuckers I know of, and add on the most corrupt too. Like Pedro from 89th, a small time dealer, got snuffed by two of them the other day with five bundles (a hundred and twenty-five bags) of fivers and I saw him today out on bail and he was rapping the scene: Like in the car on the way to getting booked the narcs were rapping right out loud to each other how much they should give in for evidence and what they ought to keep to sell for themselves back onto the street. When his case came up, it turned out they turned in one bundle for evidence, just enough to get Pedro on a selling charge and enough so they got 80% for themselves to sell to their man out on the street. So the next time you dudes smoking pipes next to a fireplace in Westchester County ask why the pusher always has plenty of dope to sell no matter how many busts are made it's because your friendly narcotic agent is filtering the shit right back out to them old street corners before you blink your know-nothing eyes.

FALL 65

Up in the country for the weekend and took some L.S.D. again with a friend at midnight. All night we walked on dirt roads and fields lit only by moon and star glow and I watched the trees to see which were friendly and which were evil. We could tell easily, and sat finally near a beautiful willow and watched its sad sway and its special glow hours until morning. At dawn light came in shafts and led me to some fields nearby to watch the tall reeds wave and then become fingers calling me over. I rolled in the dew drenched things as though they were lifting me across and through them with the fingers and my body did no work at all, in fact, I forgot all about any body I had and left it behind finally, thinking I was just a spirit flashing incredibly fast all through, wiping up the dew invisibly. I must have been there for hours and finally realized I had rolled far from the wild grass and was in the middle of a public golf course rolling for a good time while bunches of men were watching me like a moron. I saw them stare and just got up and smiled and walked off and found Willie again still near the tree, but he said the tree was very sad so we left and came back here to his little white room for music.

FALL 65

My chick from the snooty Professional Children's School, Lisa Cornbly, met me outside school today as I was making it over to Central Park for touch football gym class. It's nice watching all these fellow class saps slobber over my foxy chick, but it was a bad scene for me. I looked like king jock in these baggy sweat pants I got on and she kept goofing on me about it. I'll fix her ass later, starve her from my body for a few days or something.

For now she says she got to do some shopping and makes plans to meet me after class. Meanwhile she walks me over to the game, lagging behind so that all the rest are already doing exercises with coach Doolittle by the time I get into sight. Then Lisa makes a bitch of smart ass goof. She pulls me behind a tree and socks her tongue in my mouth and grinds her sweet bottom up against me, then suddenly a hand up my leg and grabbing my gizmo as she's still whipping that tongue. She got what she wanted, the cute little bitch, I had a hard-on like a crow bar and that's not all 'cause I forgot my jock today and didn't even wear any underwear or shit so like I was balls naked under them sweats and my prick was sticking out of them like I was shoplifting bananas. She was in stitches. Doolittle was pissed and yelling for me. She split and over I go to join the rest feebly trying to hide my still stiff wang. Now for punishment for being late I got to lie flat on my back and do forty sit-ups. I tried to think of an old lady's varicose veins to lose the stiff but it stood firm. Maybe old ladies' varicose veins turn me on, but that's another story.

FALL 65

It's an amazing thing with all the freaked out bashes and singing and goings-on up at Headquarters we weren't evicted a year ago. As is, until last night, we never even got a single noise complaint. But it was up to 110 decibels at this party for Shlink's "going into the army" last night, so much that we realized the man might bust in and wisely ruled that all dope smoking be restricted to the back room. Every fucking dope head in upper Manhattan was there, guys we never saw before are face down in the bathtub on scag or downers; in the kitchen a giant plastic garbage can filled with incredible varieties of booze and fruit punch, laced with a heaping dose of acid. Spades, whites, P.R.s, junkies, old men drunks never before seen at H.Q. stuffing any secret bologna sandwiches in their ratty coats and guzzling from the garbage can, constantly refilled. Dudes stumbling out of the back smoking room with dumb smiles, whacked on hash and grass . . . Mancole and I had to go up to the roof landing to shoot up our H because too many moochers were bugging us for "just a little taste." Actually, on the whole, just another typical Friday night up here but this time our luck gone, literally, bust. At about midnight, two blueboys showed up for a noise complaint and strolled halfway in. They popped eyes at the assortment of raggamuffins, but didn't hassle much except the usual "If we got to walk up them stairs again on your account we're going to slam you all down to the precinct," then they looked over the chicks and asked ages and proof, kicked a few youngies out (they came back as soon as the bulls split) and then tipped off. Luckily they discriminately asked no proof from the guys and double lucky did not check out the back room (where some paranoid stoned pricks made it out the window and up to the roof), or others froze or took coats to fan the smell out the window . . . Luckily no assholes dumped the dope as has happened often before out of dumb "Peter Paranoia" breathing whispers down their brains. So by this time a bunch of the unknowns had enough and split and no more complaints; I nodding in a corner through most of the whole gig, next morning I woke up on the couch with four other cats, the floor full with creeps in every position. In the kitchen, a head there face down in a pool of mustard (fortunately we pulled him out before he went down for the third time!). Even two guys in a closet, and that same stranger not budged an inch in the bathtub. But the punchline was pulled by Mancole in the afternoon when the majority floundered out and we were just watching the tube in a sea of garbage. He saw that the new woman next door (the one who no doubt phoned the complaint last night) was having a cute little birthday party for her daughter, about three or four or so, with all these little tots we see through the peekhole in the hallway, wearing cute frilly dresses holding their gifts and ringing the bell. Eventually the door was left open and we watched the cake and ice cream and pin the tail on the donkey scene. So wildman Mancole does what but, yep, calls up the fuzz and issues a very straight sounding noise complaint, "must be some rowdy teenagers drunk or maybe even smoking marriage-a-wanna, officer." A cruel prick, that Mancole, but we had to laugh our balls off as we watched the two cops storm up to the bell and ring and have these little girls holding cake and changing smiles to total stares of panic at the big blue creeps. The moms came out and yelled shit at the badges, who were five shades pink. "You should be ashamed," says the mommy. "That will fix both her and their asses," giggles Mancole, trying to get a hit on a mainline.

FALL 65

I had a tab of L.S.D. with Marc Clutcher and Anton Neutron last night, it seems it's getting to be a regular weekend thing: just like everyone else goes and gets drunk on Friday night, we gobble a tab. It was smooth and fine, just walking around St. Mark's Place playing on kazoos and digging the streets filled with goofy beautiful faces. Parking our asses outside the record store there listening to some sparks fly out of an unknown album of jazz . . . *literal* sparks, all around as that music ran. Anyway, *we knew we were there*. Where? So as usual whenever I take a tab I start digging the architecture . . . hard edges dividing city and sky, just to notice the cornices and funky gargoyles you never saw the thousand times you passed them.

Later, it gets cold, but no one is home. Can't let the wind blow our trip, I remember this guy that lives in a brownstone on 12th St., a friend of Deborah Duckster, the debutante . . . they go to school together at the Professional Children's School. He's an artist, "I'm an artist, too!" So we hustle over to the brownstone where he lives and buzz the buzz machine over his mailbox. He comes down and lets us in but I realize by his face that he don't know me as good as I thought he did. In fact, I don't think he knows me at all, so I introduce myself and my friends . . . "we take the little pill . . . feel good, radiant, dig? . . . streets get cold . . . we want refuge." He lets us up to his tiny room, baffled but we turn him on to some good grass and all's well and we listen to his great record collection, watching the fish swim around his giant tank, which is a weird scene indeed. I stare one down a long moment and he suddenly turns transparent: finally all I see is a bunch of bones moving through water.

At midnight our host tells us there's going to be a total eclipse of the moon in a few minutes and we ought to make it up to the roof to watch. What a cosmic bonus this is, I'm reeling with joy leading the way up to the roof. Trouble is that when I reach the top floor I didn't notice the ladder that you had to climb to reach the roof and, instead, thinking it's the way up, I pushed open another door and find a young German couple sitting on their living room floor watching TV. Now I was baffled plenty, "This is not a roof," I thought, trying to convince myself. I finally realized something was wrong and just looked at them, said that there was about to be a total eclipse of the moon and how they really shouldn't miss it and ran out and up the ladder. A night up there clear as windy music. I had always thought the sky was flat, but now I realized it was a friendly dome, watching secret U.F.O.s zipping over the horizon. And the eclipse was fantastic, I watched it in slow motion and understood it.

FALL 65

Last evening at about 5:15 a couple of hundred million people got their minds blown completely to shit. Within five minutes practically the entire East Coast's electrical power went pop! Listen here: I got out of basketball practice at five, then made a quick take to the subway with Lang. We just catch the last car of the Seventh Ave. local and all is cool until we get out of the tunnel at

THE BASKETBALL DIARIES | 135

125th St. and the fucking bitch starts going put-put. It's
that way on through the tunnel toward 137th St. stop
and finally, zapp, no movement, and no light, except
for the dim battery-run jobs. Everyone is mumbling the
usual blah blah about the fucked-up train system and
due to rush hour that meant a lot of blah blah 'cause
this train was packed ass to ass. Now, I waited in tunnels
before for breakdowns but around this point it's getting
to be half an hour and the place smells like a cattle car.
Everyone, it seemed, took off their coats and jackets at
the same time and rushes of stench almost blew me
down. I remembered I had been saving one last fiver of
scag in my jacket lining and I figured if this shit's keeping
up then I'm getting down. Lang and I were starting to
goof in stage whispers, "Only ten minutes of oxygen to
go," but now it's nearly an hour gone by and frankly the
war-baby-blues were starting to unscrew me, like you
don't break down an hour and more for no reason, and
I figured if this tin can went plunk we'd at least be led
out along the rails . . . plus the fact there were no tunnel
lights on either made for more A-bomb paranoia.

Finally I noticed people from the cars in front of us
moving up cars and I signaled Lang, who is nodding on
the three sniffs I turned him on to, and we head up
with some people still waiting and some following. I
figured someone must be getting out or the first car was
gonna be a human can of *Spam* for Christ sake. Anyway
we get up there and find out that out of sheer assy luck
the first door of the first car had, I swear on my moms,
made it into the station before we konked out. This was
a break but also pissed us heavily 'cause why the fuck
the big wait? Dopey mothers, these tinker toy train lames,
they wait while we sweat our balls, a woman, I saw her,

literally fainting, and me paranoid a shit war was cooking. If I wasn't buzzing a bit from junk, I might have flipped, no shit. I've always had a large fear of dead subways, second only to the bomb.

So it's up the stairs and to the street and we're looking around, a fire truck right there for some trash can smoking in the playground, big deal, and I ask some old donkey Irishman, "What's up, train power failure?" "Whole goddamn city is blacked out, laddie," he answers in thick brogue. "Whole East Coast up to Canada! I heard on the transistor," another cat in neat big suit, pipes in. I look around with Lang and can't believe it . . . no street lights, no billboards, not one light in the whole row of tenements across the street, but for one candle dim on a third floor window. What the cosmic fuck is this? I hear it for myself in this crowd around a dude with a transistor. The thing was true: *all N.Y.C.* plus most of the coast all the way up. I peeked across a dark Hudson River to some high-rises in Jersey and they still had power . . . which relieved me a bit 'cause I was getting the Commie Conspiracy-here-comes-the-big-one blues more and more. I asked Lang about that and he brushed it and said be cool, only problem now is getting home. Less a mess for him there 'cause he lived on 150th and Riverside in a big posh black bourgeois building, right across the hall from "The Shirelles." I told him to squeeze into this packed bus, I'd hitch or shit; and he tips into the back door and buzzes. I got a big bag filled with books I took home tonight (my luck) and dirty gym laundry for washing. Seventy-five blocks from home, but a news-truck pulls up and shouts, "Going as far as 181st, hop in the back." I buzz my ass in, no way me being polite, on the nod with seventy-five blocks to walk. There we go, a few office girls, white collar lames, a spade wino just along for the ride . . . and me, our asses banging around on stacks of the "NY Post." This cat was wheeling good, had to hang on tight, some foxy office doll clutching me every which way. "Crazzzeeee-est thing I ever HAVE seen in all my days," she repeats to everyone in deep down-home drawl, giant fake eyelashes flickering madly. Up the big hill to 181st and out we go, still a ways off but all downhill from here on . . . buses too packed and a hundred frantics in line . . . fuck that. I look around and cop a brain buzz. "Food Carnival" right across the street seeming all locked up but delivery bikes still outside, no locks. I mad dash onto one, the kind with the big box in the front with three wheels, and I'm in the wind turning down Broadway, my case of books and dirty laundry in the box and some fat Italian guy, the manager I assume, in a desperate fat-man trot in futile pursuit. What a blast, all steep hill to 200th Street and straight on from there. It's cold, but I'm making time and buzzing. I leave it in front of the pizza joint a few blocks away, walk to my house, hit the church across the street for some free candles, feel my way up the stairs by candle light and pile some lamb chops down, getting the rest of the family stories, none near mine for sheer adventure. I got to say it was some lucky breaks I got. House well lit by candles.

So my brother and I go out and dig the streets and all the guys are out, some throwing out the Russians-did-it theory which I forgot by now, but all agreeing tonight's the night to break into the park house again for some new basketballs and footballs and shit. You bet it was: we could have easily done a bigger job I'll bet . . . every cop was busy with traffic and emergencies, not a soul in the park. We crowbarred the door, found a giant sack and got some beauties (even a goddamn shuffle board set), and, to boot, found a fifth of booze in Rufus the park man's locker and sat cool and polished that (I held off, I copped another bag of H and got my gimmicks and shot up for once in the park without cop paranoia). Split them, hid the stuff in the woods, and some guys went to Forster's for beers (the old bugger stayed open using candles on the bar); I just went home and nodded, an interesting day, light and dark.

FALL 65

Being a big time basketball star and all around hip motherfucker at a private school, I get to meet a lot of out of sight private school chicks, all of them action and plenty rich to boot. I went to visit my current girlfriend, Hedi Hunter, today because it's Friday and every Friday her parents go out for big night on the town leaving the apartment to just Hedi and me and about fifty maids and butlers. She lives over on Sutton Place overlooking the East River in an eighteen-room penthouse . . . Her old man is a big wheel at MGM or something and her old lady owns mucho race horses and stuff like that. I wouldn't mind putting a little make on her moms as a matter of fact, she's early forties but still in great shape. So anyway, I tool in and nod to the doorman who knows me by now and lets me right up without the casual C.I.A. bit they usually give you in these places. The elevator cat is a tall spade who used to play semi-pro ball so we rap a lot until I reach the top, get out, give a ring, flip my beret to Harry, the butler, and get greeted by Hedi, all sexy in her great dress. We eat a little Italian food in the dining room, then go up to her room which pans right out over the river with its slow barges and ugly boroughs that surround it. I whip out a little hash and she tosses me her excellent pipe and in ten minutes the view is an awful lot more pleasing outside. Construction is some heavy stuff over in Long Island City, all those huge girders just sticking up in that old sky like air knives. But enough for the view and we wrap up for some great nookie and muff away for an hour or two. I never get tired of this scene though I've been coming here for the last two months. The rest of the night we just sit around on Hedi's big bed naked and watch goofy Peter Sellers movies on big color TV. I show her action shot of me in *The Times* while scoring forty against McBurney yesterday. She beams and we fuck again. It's a goof, all this stuff. I'm gonna bring all the dirt heads from old Madison Square Boy's Club up here some night: they'll freak out in one second. Finally I realize that I got to meet some friends uptown soon so I split about midnight after checking out what pills I can rob out of her old man's medicine cabinet. I got about eight ups and a lot of downers. I give Hedi the big kiss, munch on a pear and cut out.

FALL 65

The real culprits in the nonending rift between my old man and me is neither one of us, I've realized. No doubt in my mind it's the assorted big-mouthed bergs of shit that float in and out of the joint that he sweats his ass off tending bar in all day . . . "The customers," as he puts it, "your bread and butter!" For all their jobs as cops and construction workers, for all their crewcuts and their "Bomb Hanoi Now!" buttons these all-American jokes gossip away suspiciously worse than the most overt fags on Greenwich Ave. They constantly lean over the bar in giggly whispers . . . "Hey, what the hell is with your son with all that hair down to his shoulders and those funny clothes he wears, I thought he was a big star ballplayer . . . he ain't one of them an-ti-war creeps, huh? What the hell they telling him in that fancy pinko school he goes to, huh? huh? . . . I mean, Christ, you oughta have a talk with him, huh? yer know? I mean, Jesus . . ." These peckers are the types I can imagine give their wife bread to go out on Sunday so they can dress up in the old lady's underwear, turn on the game and dig themselves in full-length mirrors in drag while grown men score touchdowns on TV to get to pat each other on the ass. I doubt none of these speculations.

FALL 65

A note found on one of those little homework pads you cop for ten cents at Gussie's . . . I wrote on an experience with L.S.D. a while ago:

> "Little kids shoot marbles
> where the branches break the sun
>
> into graceful shafts of light . . .
> I just want to be pure."

I found it all crumbled up in these old pants in history class this morning.

FALL 65

Junkies are a strange lot, you begin to wonder after a while. I mean tonight everybody down at the park is raving on the dynamite stuff that this dude Fudgy is doing and warning all of us not to score from Fat Victor who is right there in front of us, not ten feet away: "Strictly garbage next to Fudgy's, let's find him." Shit, no, not me, I ain't done any scag in a month or so now and I dig the convenience of Victor, so I cop three fivers and take to the bushes to get off. I get wrecked, it's plenty good, but, no, the other cats got to take off to dig out Fudgy down near the poolroom. Now he's down dealing on the hottest corner in the city, like a furnace that street, can feel narco heat waves through your sneakers down there. Then there's the wait, first for Fudgy to make his entrance (he knows he got the best, he knows they're gonna wait), then he got to collect the money and run up to his apartment in the projects to pick up. Much too hot to carry these days down there. Add that to the fact that I wouldn't trust Fudgy to cop me an aspirin, if he gets enough bread up he may not be back for a week. There's always an excuse, like he got busted and beat it but they took the dope and he had to do a week at Riker's. He did it to me before. So to make tonight's story short, eight guys went down and they all got pulled in for loitering right after they put out their last bread. So they'll have a nice sick night in the tombs and they'll be lucky if Fudgy pays them back. Meanwhile, I'm nodding, no hassles.

But Willie and Billy didn't get slammed by the man and they come back with their shots. I'm zonked on the swings in the playground slugging Pepsi as they come in to get some water to take up the hill to shoot up. I got one bag left and I join them. Now there's one set of gimmicks hid up there and it's the filthiest spike you ever could see, been used by guys I prefer not to think of out of the fact my stomach is a bit upset. But you bet your ass there is not one bit of hesitation in drawing your shot into that harpoon and shoving it into your mainline. If you got dope you will get it inside you no matter how and I will too I can't deny that. But here's what I can't get. Willie asks me for a slug of soda so I pass him the bottle and what the hell does he do but pull that old second grade bullshit of wiping off the top of the bottle before he takes some. Shit, I mean anything I can give him from that bottle he's gonna get a lot easier from using the same spike. None of these lames think twice, or once, in fact. They remind me of a girl I slept with last week who almost sleeps with her tongue in my mouth (besides a lot of other places too) and the next morning gets uptight about me using her fucking toothbrush. But, you know, I can get their point thinking about it, because when that ugly bastard Willie handed me back my soda I took one look at his drooling mug and tossed the rest of the thing away.

FALL 65

Jimmy Mancole and I came within inches of getting our
asses tossed in the can tonight. We beat some dopey
private school chicks I know for ten beans pawning off
a bag of dill weed from momma's spice cabinet as grass
and talked this spade dealer into letting us light $2 for
two sixers. This guy is always straight with something
good and we were lucky to score off him 'cause he usually sells out by evening and we got the last two about
nine. I run over to get a cup of water from the deli and
Mancole goes ahead into the park and gets the works
we hide behind a brick in back of the park house. We
make it up to the usual spot near the Cloisters, find a
twist-off beer cap for a cooker and cook up. I get off
first and get smashed on the rush, real top grade stuff,
then just as Jimmy is cooked and trying to find a mainline we hear one of these new motorbikes the cops are
now using heading down the trail toward us. We're right
under a lamp post to see what we're doing but that's the
shit about getting off in the park. Got one thing to do
and that's make a leap off the wall about a ten feet drop
before the scooter hits around the bend and spots us. I
do it without thinking and almost break my fucking
ankle, then drops Mancole with, dig it, the spike still
in his arm landing on top of me. I almost blew up at
the fuck but I stayed cool and Mr. putt-putt went putt-
putting right by. Then we look up and Mancole notices
that as he fell he hit a vein and the blood is filling the
dropper, craziest fucking hit I ever saw anyone get. He
put it in and booted once. All this time I'm up and
limping on a swollen ankle and rubbing the arm that he
fell on. I'm also vowing to find a safer place to get off,

but since big Joe took the overdose at Headquarters, it's been a rule no one shoots dope up there . . . just smoking, and we ain't got another house and it would look a bit fucked up picketing Headquarters for grass heads being unrightful to junkies. I guess it's the park or nothing, unless I can cut loose, which I ought to be doing soon 'cause it's starting to get heavy, starting to be that time I better get my ass together.

FALL 65

That cop that has been patrolling the park on his little putt-putt motorbike and busting people for smoking grass and shooting dope got hustled last night. Some cats I know tied a real taut metal wire across a dark part of a little path hoping to cut the man's head off. The one thing they forgot was the fact that he got a windshield on his bike. It fucked him up anyway though, it knocked the bike out of control and he took a bad spill and busted a leg or some shit. That scene screws up everyone now 'cause they got cops like ants out all over that park and if you're picked up there you're as good as down to the station no questions asked. One rule is not to fuck up the man 'cause they come in swarms busting everyone's balls if you do.

FALL 65

Lately my scene at home has dissolved to total bullshit. What to say? My old man gets home at six every day, eats, takes off his shoes and sits in his chair with his pants rolled up and his varicose veins sticking out with his feet up on the stool and he bitches. He bitches about how my hair's too long, that the protesters suck, about nigger this and spic that, the same old shit and I don't answer 'cause he don't listen anyway. It's all so simple it's the most complicated shit I ever had to put up with. Then I got my old lady always trying to bait me into political debates as soon as the news pops on and if I bite and argue then the whole house is a screaming maniac nut house and if I don't bother it's even worse. And I don't bother anymore. I just refuse to give the slightest fuck anymore and o.k. if I'm all fucked up and, yes, every other race, creed & color sucks and the war in Nam is sanctioned by the Pope who is flawless of course and if I could just bend in half I could suck myself off all day and load up on some good scag and live in a closet because you can't beat them but you can ignore and induce ulcers and heart pangs and give them grey hair so to drive them stone bust on beauty parlor tint-up jobs and then you begin to cry in the closet because your veins are sore and you can't get over the fact that you love them somehow more or at least always.

FALL 65

I think today was about the last peace march I'm gonna make, fucking things are just one big bore. Like they got these "Marshalls" telling you how you gotta keep in straight lines and all and that's the shit that we're marching against in the first place. Who needs leaders? Leaders should be kicked in the ass and packaged airmail to some cornfield in Kansas . . . they are not needed. If I'm not on my own in something I'm doing, it's time to split. Have a goof on these marches says me, grab an ass or roller skate or piss on Macy's corner stone. All this serious rap, stone faces and crap are a drag. Most of the cats marching are only there to get laid anyway, and no body in that fucking Pentagon is getting the hint, so maybe it's time to fling a few bricks around instead of boring speeches, we need more street people kicking and biting instead of a bunch of walking boots. Time to change the way of getting the message across, it's all such a drag anyway.

WINTER 1966

WINTER 1966

WINTER 66

I'm gonna *do it* soon, if I could only get my hands on one I know I could slip it out of my bag and make Swiss cheese out of this place. I mean my English class at school, my first class in the morning.... didn't I talk about it before, my fantasy that always creeps on my back when I'm sitting there each morning ... just wanting to whip out a tommy gun and blast away (Nothing less will do, no pistols, nothing else besides rat-a-tat-tat, dig?). Well it seems to be getting to be more than a fantasy lately, and I don't have a buzz to a clue why? Like I say it's my first class, see ... and before we hit school most days we stop in at this chick, Judy, who lives right up the block on Central Park West, and we smoke a little dope, or shoot up etc., whatever your taste. So by the time I get into class I'm so tired and nodding and this puppet up at the blackboard is busy telling us something about how it doesn't take away from Whitman's poetry even if he was a fag or some other tidbit of interest and my eyes drift slowly up and it's all just a landscape of cracked, yellow clay with barbed wire and trenches and miles of blackboard glaring with the enemy heat and I begin to cut up that scene with my m.g. and all until suddenly I'm back in that same classroom with the puppet up there lecturing again, just as boringly real as ever. I mean if I could just get it off once ... just really cut the place to ribbons ... just for once ...

WINTER 66

I was just rising out of the subway at Dyckman St. this evening after copping a bundle down at the poolhall on 53rd and there I see fat Henry standing in the middle of a goddamn six-way intersection, blasted like his eyes are two thin red slits, with a plastic whistle in his hands and a ridiculous sea captain's hat on his head, directing traffic. He was within inches of getting his ass sliced off in every direction and the cars are backed up, shit, what do you say? I was uptight to help him 'cause of the heat I was carrying but I made it to Headquarters, and sent G-Burger down to get him but by the time G gets his coat on Moochie walks in and tells us we should have seen this fat jerk with a plastic whistle etc. getting hauled away just a minute ago. No class at all, that blimp, worst dope fiend in the city won't be caught dead with him.

WINTER 66

I'm not as afraid of the bomb as I was a couple of years ago but there's still plenty of paranoia left . . . no doubt about that. It's just that I've gradually let it grow into a subtle way of life . . . it's gotten down to a matter of counting the days . . . buying time in between each new cold war flare-up. You buy on fear as credit. I was thinking about it today.

I was thinking about how I can divide my past into lumps of time in which I had myriad, "important" reasons to wish (and earlier, say from seven to nine or so, to pray) that the end of the world, that the pushing of the button would wait just a little while longer until each of these particular "reasons to hang on a bit longer" had seen itself through. "Just let this one project I got going for me make it before the end," I remember thinking, "it will only take four more months or so . . . then if the fucking place is gonna go, let 'er rip!" The project didn't have to be a huge one, and the time always varied. Age eight: hoping that the big shots could cool it, could postpone the bomb one summer, so I could play just one whole season in my first year in little league baseball before the end. Even, I can dig it, just hoping we could delay taking action in the Cuban crisis so I'd play in a really important basketball game on a Friday night. The time we were supposed to go to that out of sight Boys' Club camp, age nine, if we could get through that month that summer before the end . . . because this is no bullshit, where I am coming from . . . this is the way I measured my future time . . . there was no way you could think of one without the other . . . every time a big trip was coming up, or the season was starting in some sport . . . anything that was worth looking ahead to, well, that's when it always seemed the sirens were gonna start the death chant.

But it's not at all just something that's past and solved. Not at all. It's just that I can see it a little clearer now, that fear is their tool . . . and it works very well . . . and they use it very well. And I still am using it to measure my time, only I don't give a screw about trips to camp anymore, or basketball games two weeks from now. It's just gotten bigger now . . . will I have time to finish the poems breaking loose in my head? Time to find out if I'm the writer I know I can be? How about these diaries? Or will Vietnam beat me to the button? Because it's poetry now . . . and the button is still there, waiting . . .

WINTER 66

I went to a going away party tonight in this local bar that all the big brothers of my uptown friends hang out in. We weren't supposed to be in there of course because of our age but there's this guy around here that sells perfect fake draft cards so we were all guzzling away and all, getting pretty smashed. The party was for Blue-boy's big brother Gums, who is sucked into the army machine in the morning. Blue-boy and Gums are two of the biggest rednecks in this redneck neighborhood and they're always putting me down 'cause I'm against the war but I make this scene anyway 'cause there ain't nothing else happening around here. So after everyone got half a bag on, the scene turns into a real Hollywood winner. Gums's old man secretly turns off the jukebox & sneaks around and tells everyone to pitch in for a chorus of "Danny Boy" (Gums's real name). This corn ass shit actually comes off and in the middle of everyone singing Gums runs up in tears to his old man and gives him this giant hug and then does the same drama with his brother. It was the most pathetic ball of corn I've ever seen, bar none. And from that point on the gang continues with "My Country 'Tis Of Thee" and "America" etc, etc . . . Audie Murphy never got anything like this, I'm standing there trying to figure out if this is real. But then Fat Eddie delivers the clincher to me, he tells me that Gums is only going in for a six month bit in the reserves over on Staten Island and that's the closest he'll ever get to Vietnam. We were laughing so hard that some of the people even stopped singing to see what was happening. Now there's a family that knows how to make a mountain out of a pile of shit, what a sense of

drama. Damn, from the scene here you'd think old Gums
had to assassinate Chairman Mao with a water pistol.
I'm glad I'm on the other side 'cause chumps like that
are sure losers.

WINTER 66

We just got into town for the very spectacular National
High School All Star Basketball Game. The town by the
way is Washington, D.C. I got stuck in the same car as
Benny Greenbaum, the infamous queer scout from a
well-known Midwestern University, and the fuck kept
playing with my hair all the way down. We stopped at
three different Howard Johnson's on the route but I'm
still plenty hungry. This team looks in pretty sad shape;
Larry Newbold was supposed to meet us at the corner
of 116th and Lenox but he never showed up. This doesn't
bother me too much because now I'll be the starting
guard. Benny asks me if I want to be his roommate for
$25 a night and I probably would have been until Joe
Slapstick, the coach, told Benny to fuck off to another
motel. Instead I get stuck with shithead Bobby Bellum,
a real jockstrap who came down in a station wagon with
his whole family. He hates me but he took me as a room
mate because his father won't let him sleep with a spade
and I'm the only other white man.

  In the evening we're supposed to watch very spectacular films of last year's game but fuck that. Bax Porter,
this real light skinned spade, and I climb out of his
window to get laid in the dark section of town. Porter's
a great player. I once saw him take a silver dollar from

the top of the backboard and he's only about 6′5″. He's also a great guy and he had me fixed up with this very fine spade chick. She said she liked my long hair so I told her I was a sensitive young artist, as well, who wrote spirited poems of varying length. She asked me if I knew Allen Ginsberg. I told her everybody in N.Y. knew Allen Ginsberg. Not too bright Bax thought Allen was another queer Jew basketball scout like Benny Greenbaum. It was a great lay. We didn't make it back to our room until about midnight and Joe Slapstick was waiting around for our asses. He told us we couldn't even get dressed for the game two nights from now. Bullshit. We both knew we would be starting. There just wasn't enough guys on the team to kick us off. Who gave a shit about the game anyway? I had plenty of dope and that great little black ass downtown. Slapstick told us to take a shower and nod off. We had two joints each in the shower and went back to my room. Bax beat the ass off Bobby Bellum for squeaking to the coach that we were late, I read "Music" by Frank O'Hara and began thinking about the Plaza Hotel. That poem always reminds me of the Plaza Hotel.

WINTER 66

After a very poor breakfast Joe Slapstick calls aside Bax and me and lets us know he is giving us another chance and we would be starting in the game anyway. Benny Greenbaum comes in and plays with my ear and tells me all about the man I'll be guarding on the next night. The man I'm guarding happens to be Art Baylor, a cousin of Elgin Baylor who's my favorite player. Benny says the guy drives a lot and I should keep one leg in his crotch just before he starts to drive. Benny demonstrates and rubs his knee against my balls.

After Benny has demonstrated on every player on the team, someone discovers that Sammy Fulton, a center from Clinton, has incredible amounts of very up pills. We all go to practice stoned. I hit incredible amounts of jump shots in practice and assure myself a starting spot in the game. I practiced passing off because I figured I'd be a playmaker if nothing else. Ben Davis hurt his leg and is out for the whole tournament. I read in the Washington newspapers a story about me entitled "Beatnik Basketball Player" telling all about my shoulder length hair and my strange hobbies off the court. What the fuck is this all about? I get a great urge to nod out despite the pills. I'm about to go into the room when Joe Slapstick stops me and tells me that I should run the offense because Porter is too dumb. Bellum and his old man are in the room as I get there. They're probably talking about the story in today's paper. I'm sure he hates the idea of a creep like me starting in the game. Bullshit. I sweated my nuts off for that spot so he can go fuck himself.

WINTER 66

Coming back from the Washington trip today, we stopped at a gas station in Benny's car and Yogi went behind the place to use the bathroom. Corky and I went inside to use the Coke machine and used a few of the handy slugs that he had brought along for such situations. Back to the car in a few minutes, Yogi comes whipping out of the bathroom with this big smile on his face. "Probably just beat off, the sneaky fuck," someone crudely observed, but Yogi came running over to the car saying, "Heh, there's a scumbag machine in the bathroom in there." "What the fuck are you talking about," Willie asked. "I swear they got a scumbag machine in there," and he took out and dangled one large, sure enough, scumbag in front of us. "Pretty great, eh?" "What a goof," I said, and we all ran around the back to check it out, Benny included. There it was, 25¢ a pack. I never saw a scumbag machine before in N.Y. but somebody explained that they had them in every bathroom in every filling station in the South. Corky put in a quarter and waited for the prize but nothing happened. "Slam it," someone contributed, and he pounded very hard on the top of the machine. It freaked our minds as the whole bottom of the thing came out and thousands of packs of scumbags fell onto the floor. We got down on hands and knees to pick them all up and shove them into our pockets knowing they would be big sellers to all the lames in our school who didn't have the balls to go into a drugstore and ask for a pack. In fact, dumb old Corky croaked, "Well, wouldn't you be uptight to go into a drugstore and say, 'Three scumbags please.' " We took a little time out to explain a few facts to Corky.

Meanwhile, Benny seemed right at home in the bathroom and took the opportunity to try to deal some blowjobs to us. No one considered the scene very cool for shit like that so, after we checked to make sure we had all the rubbers off the floor, we made it back to the car. Benny sagged back in disappointment and once we got started again the fuck nearly cracked us up into a truck. "Get your mind off my dick and back on the road," said Willie and it zonked me out when we all looked over into the front seat to see his pants down to his ankles and him rubbing Johnson and Johnson's baby powder onto his balls. "Jock-rash," he explained. "Oh," I nodded. We sniffed a little junk in the back seat so the next few hours were not too literary for the diary but plenty pleasant for the old head. In Baltimore, however, we did run into Corky's cousin in a little food shop. I think she was a fucking whore or something. They rapped for a while and we split, a very touching reunion. When we were about an hour from the city, everyone started to blow up the scumbags and send them out the window. At a food stand we gave a few blow ups to a little girl and her mother. "Take the balloons from the nice boys," she said, dumb New Jersey housewife jive.

WINTER 66

Back a day now from that crazy trip to Washington so Benny calls me up on the phone and tells me that he wants me to play on his team, *The Flyers*, and that I should come over to his big beautiful apartment to get fitted for one of those famous *Flyer* uniforms and get a free pair of expensive sneakers to boot. I ask if I might meet him at some safer place, but he assures me it's cool up there, so I get dressed and start over. When I got there it was really on one of those plush streets and it had a doorman. After the C.I.A. treatment from the old lady at the switchboard in the lobby I walk up sixteen flights of stairs (because I have this fear of elevators you see), and get to the door and ring the bell. Benny answers with this big here's-my-little-darling-now smile on his face and we go and sit in the living room and have a Coke a minute or two and then he gets up and signals me into the next room to try on the uniform. Once we got into this little bedroom in the back, Benny told me to sit down on the bed. I waited while he got a very flashy warmup jacket out of the closet and I tried it on. It fit perfectly over my thin body and he started to rub his palms over my chest and took it back off me and then he looked at me and said, "Take off your pants and try on these bottoms," so I unzipped my boots and took off my blue jeans and threw them over the arm of the chair next to me and he handed me the shorts and told me that I shouldn't wear any underwear when I tried them on because the fit might not be right. I hesitated a minute. "Holy shit," I thought, "what the fuck have you gotten yourself into," and I was really nervous whether to punch this guy or take off the pants and be cool and try on the shorts. But he stopped me and told me that he wanted to take my measurements first. Then he sort of took my body and laid it against the wall and began to measure my thighs and my calf muscles (13 inches by the way) and then the fucker did it. He pressed his fingers very softly against my prick and my balls and said that now we should measure that. No more, I thought. I took that motherfucker and, mostly by instinct I guess, gave him a pretty solid fiver across the back of his neck. He was face down on his knees now from the punch, so I just took him by the face and pushed him so his head hit on the brass bed post and then I simply whipped my clothes back on (picked up the uniform) and made it to the door where he came running after me and told me not to be angry, that it didn't matter, that he thought I was cute and couldn't help himself from at least trying me, that he was sincere and thought he might even be in love with me and that we could see each other all summer and go to drive-in movies or something like that. Holy shit what the fuck was this guy all about? Well, he gave me $20 not to say anything and to be friends and all that and (you bet your sweet ass) I took the bread and split, shaking like the old bugger's prick, and I made it into the elevator because I was freaked out that I even forgot that I was afraid of elevators.

WINTER 66

The more I read the more I know it now, heavier each day, that I need to write. I think of poetry and how I see it as just a raw block of stone ready to be shaped, that way words are never a horrible limit to me, just tools to shape. I just get the images from the upstairs vault (it all comes in images) and fling 'em around like bricks, sometimes clean and smooth and then sloppy and ready to fall on top of you later. Like this house where I got to sometimes tear out a room and make it another size or shape so the rest make sense ... or no sense at all. And when I'm done I'm stoned as on whatever you got in your pockets right now, dig?

Now I got these diaries that have the greatest hero a writer needs, this crazy fucking New York. Soon I'm gonna wake a lot of dudes off their asses and let them know what's really going down in the blind alley out

there in the pretty streets with double garages. I got a
tap on all your wires, folks. I'm just really a wise ass kid
getting wiser and I'm going to get even somehow for
your dumb hatreds and all them war baby dreams you
left in my scarred bed with dreams of bombs falling
above that cliff I'm hanging steady to. Maybe someday
just an eight-page book, that's all, and each time a page
gets turned a section of the Pentagon goes blast up in
smoke. Solid.

WINTER 66

I brought a few guys down from uptown tonight and
we ran a little game against some old black friends of
mine in this cheesebox of a gym on 127th Street. We
didn't really keep any score but it was a good workout
anyway and after we were dressed and heading for the
subway Ronnie Jackson offered to buy us some drinks
in this little dive off Eighth Avenue. First we made it to
Riverside Drive and blew a few joints in the cold river
wind and make our way over to his hangout zonked. We
get some queasy stares from one or two dudes in the
place but Ronnie knows them a bit so he assures them
and us that everything is cool. It's only been a week or
so now that the latest riots broke out here in Harlem so
you can't help walking around with the feeling of secret
guns pointed at you from somewhere above you every
other moment but since we're with some of the roughest
cats from this turf things seem pretty secure. Just the
same, if matters boiled over the way they did a week ago
I could be walking along with the ghost of Malcolm X

and they'd be opening fire anyway. I'm glad to see all the smashed in boarded-up windows of all those white crook storeowners down here all cleared out of their TVs and radios by the people who should have them for once anyway. And I hate seeing heads smashed in but I'll lay any odds there's more to come and though I'd like to help my black friends, the only thing I can do is stand aside because that's the only way they can get down on it and besides I don't dig those bullets zinging over my bean, coming from either cop or black man.

So anyway we sit and order screwdrivers and we're bullshitting when I swear on your mother two fellows bop in and whip out two very shiny revolvers and inform us that this place is being held up. We're all shitting in our pants at this point but these guys are just interested in the cash register and the bartender is cool and lays the entire contents on the bar for them. Then they come over to each of us at the bar and take in from us whatever we have to offer, not much from us in fact only fifty cents from me and they let me keep my subway token, which was nice enough of them I have to admit. One of the two, who seemed a bit more jittery than the other, wanted to take Ray's grass but the partner just stared over to him and said, "Are you crazed, sucker? We could get arrested for that shit." So finishing up at the end of the bar they reach this chubby old guy who looks like he works at the garage next door, the type that comes in for a shot of booze every other hour. The taller of the two slicks whips his hand down for the 60¢ there but the chubby dude grabs it and shouts, "No good, you punk bastards, I come in here every night at this time for a drink out of the money I work my ass off for and you ain't taking it, no you ain't!!!" "We don't want no trouble pop," says the hold-up man, "just lay that 6/10ths into my palm." These cats have to be really strung out, scraping like that for 60 fucking cents, but the old guy don't want to hear it and keeps his bread tight in his hand. "God damn it, give up that money!" "Not a chance you pricks!" At this point we were almost breaking apart on the goof with these two guys with guns and all hassling with this cocky old bastard. Now dig this: he asks the pops one more time and he still ain't giving in, so the crook walks around the bar, blows a big sigh, looks straight at the man and asks "what the hell you drinkin?" The old man beams and answers, "Canadian Club, straight." So the slick pours the shot after an angry grab at the Club bottle, whips the 60¢ off the bar, turns and tips out the door with his partner as the old weasel smiles and sips down his drink. You probably figure I made this one up, but I swear every word is true.

WINTER 66

Just such a pleasure to tie up above that mainline with a woman's silk stocking and hit the mark and watch the blood rise into the dropper like a certain desert lily I remember I saw once in my child's encyclopedia, so red . . . yeah, I shoot desert lilies in my arm.

It's been hard, the writing, lately. Just all comes in beautiful fragments, like nods now . . . so high . . . guess I'd rather sleep forever this sleep and forget . . . but the gnats, they keep buzzing in my ear and the heat and the dreams . . .

Black Earl's on the sofa, he is a man who all day just cleans his nails . . . we'll bury him with his file, dig?

Bob Dylan, he's in the radio. He glows in the dark and my fingers are just light feathers falling and fading down . . .

WINTER 66

It is common knowledge around the entire school that Marc Clutcher, Anton Neutron and myself are fucking up our basketball team by taking every drug we can get our hands on before games. It's common knowledge to the rest of the teams in the league too, mainly because we wear our hair about ten times the normal length, and drop games to lame teams by fucking around on the court and not giving a shit. Now our coach is getting wise and today, after we lost to Riverdale by two points last night, the headmaster called me into his office and told me he had a report about me taking ups before the game. The funny part about this is that yesterday was one of the few times I was straight while playing and it was simply the fact that they had three fucking butchers on me all game that I couldn't get it together. He asked me if I had ever taken a drug while I was at school and I told him it was none of his business for openers and anyway I never had and who the hell told him I did. He took my word for it for the time being but of course didn't tell me who it was that ratted on me. He didn't have to 'cause I got a pretty good idea who it is and I sent a little note in English class to the team manager Muggsy Woods that he better shut his fucking trap or he's gonna cop a little skin from the three of us. I immediately warned Marc and Anton and we cleaned out our lockers of any incriminating materials, hid them in a spare locker that we found in the visitor's locker room, and snapped on a lock. So what the fuck happens next but an assembly gathering the whole student body together and Mr. Bluster, principal, announces that the local police have heard that our school is a hot spot for drugs and that he has a warrant, issued with our headmaster's permission, to search all lockers in the building. Beads of sweat start pouring down every face in the room and after the speech is over there's a mad dash to lockers with us included. We clean out and check out a back door and hide our shit in a wastebasket in a paper bag down the street, saving a joint to blow before the game in N.J. this afternoon. Imagine the nerve of that son of a bitch letting the man come in the school like that. Panic all over faces in every grade, freshman up, and especially in ours since we're the heads of Carroll, Clutcher, and Neutron Inc. which is the main dealing outfit in the school. We decide to cool all enterprise for the time being lest some big mouth freshman stools on us. Since we're only sophomores we have to deal with keeping the upperclass cats quiet too but they assure us it's cool. What a fucking game that was today too. Shit, that new grass was mighty fine. I was so zonked that I drove clean around my man once and had an easy layup and looked up and tossed the ball right over the fucking backboard. Then I got fouled once and stood on the line just goofing on what a dumb fucking thing to be doing on a nice day like today, I stared so long the ref finally came over and asked me if I was alright. Then I burst out laughing and shot the thing about four feet short of the rim. The coach whipped me out of the game but it was near the end at least and we won anyway. I was so out of it today that even our mild mannered coach Mr. Doolittle gave me shit about being high and I hope it don't get back to that headmaster creep again. All around it was a bad day for our dealing business and a bring down game that fucked up my leading scoring average. To make it worse the dumb prick, Charlie the bus driver, got on the wrong end of the turnpike and we were almost in goddamn Pennsylvania before anyone noticed, I got home close to midnight for fuck sake.

WINTER 66

Smack across the alley from the back window of Head-quarters, where I've been living these weekends, is this tall foxy chick's bedroom window in living color. Alley couldn't be more than six feet across and it seems she ain't found out yet about the shade being invented, so it's a show every morning her dressing for work and every night taking it off again. This does not include the many bonus hours on her days off bobbing around her big naked body past the window or right in front of the mirror playing around with her perfect spoons. Bitch is naked so much in fact that I been getting sick of her lately. She's been in front of that mirror so much that I feel like kicking her out and getting someone else to move in. Perhaps a redhead for a change. I almost feel guilty bringing a chick up to my place with her there all the time, like once I brought up this chick maybe a week ago and we're in bed and I look over my shoulder and there she is combing away in the raw and I wanted to get out of bed with the chick I'm with just to watch her. You must be thinking I should shout over to her or something but, shit that would be horrible, that would ruin the whole thing.

WINTER 66

You certainly have to go to an awful lot of hassle just to visit a friend these days. I popped into the lobby of a dorm for N.Y.U. students down in the Village last night to see this chick Bunny Begalot, a freshman who cribs in this particular place. I already had her room number and all so when I walked in I headed straight for the elevator (I hate elevators as I've said before but I couldn't find the stairs). So I press the button there and, damn, did the shit ever hit the fan! A guard in uniform quickly approached me in a manner rather rude, asked my business, and hauls me over to the "Visitor's desk." I get eyed like a rag, they call up Bunny who has to describe me, I have got to show the dude my I.D. (my probation card is all I got), they make me fill out a card which they stamp in a clock device and finally escort me over to the elevator.

If you think this is any of your business, I get greeted at the door by Bunny, we smoke some grass, we fuck, we smoke some more, we fuck some more, we dig the logopoeia.

Now it's time to leave and this is where the real trouble hits. This time I find the stairs and decide to take them . . . Bunny's going out for snacks so she's with me. She thinks it's a little silly walking down eight flights of stairs but there is no chance of me getting in an elevator after smoking grass, I just mumble some shit about "back to nature" rather than admit I'm scared shit of the thing. So we reach the door that leads out to the street, big metal door like in the Tombs or some other joint. I push to open it but Bunny leaps to stop me. "Que pasa?" say I. It seems that this is some emergency door and you have to press a button next to it while you open the thing and press another button outside as you're closing it or else alarms go off all over the place. So it seems the alarms have gone off and out onto the sidewalk pour all these guards who slam me up on the wall until Bunny explains. They let me go but tell me I'm banned from the place for the rest of the year. Very strange indeed, now besides all the bullshit they give you to get in the place you have to start pressing buttons to get out for Christ sake! There's something going on here, there's some kind of significance here or something.

WINTER 66

I have an older woman that I see now very often on the weekends, she is the friend of the mother of an old girl friend of mine . . . very rich and, in a slutty way, very sexy. I heard on a TV talk show the other night a lady shrink rapping how a woman reaches her sexual peak around forty while man is at his top from about sixteen to eighteen. This would make us the perfect sex match on paper, but there's one hitch . . . Though she is without doubt at her peak of horn growth (actually she is out and out insatiable), I am, on the other hand, ready for all she wants in my head but my body is sometimes so pumped with junk when I see her that I'm only good for a couple of rounds a night. After that she's always still left rolling all over me with me just staring at the ceiling . . . or the TV if I can sneak it on. There are other problems involved. Like she has always been unable to have a child (married twice, at present separated) and I'm sure she sees me somewhere along those lines. A mutual friend told me how she shows a picture of me to unhip friends as her son. This makes for more confusion in bed. What's that? What I have here is a simple Oedipus scene? Is that what you said, Doc? But that is not the case in whole, not it at all. The confusion stems from the fact that we always wind up, after a little foreplay, putting on a grand scale production of her favorite fantasy. This is the incestuous lesbian route. I dress up in drag (and I mean she does it complete) and now mother and son are mother and daughter. But it gets more interesting than that still. In her games, *I* wind up being the mother and she's the daughter . . . so after awhile I don't know if I'm goddamn male or female, mommy or daddy, sugar or spice or puppy dog tails. What the fuck . . . at least I make one fine looking woman in those glowing originals she drapes me in.

WINTER 66

I saw my old lady lover tonight and, since I tried to keep down my junk consumption today, I was horny myself to get it on. I told her something else too. I told her I was sick of dressing up in drag for her and I didn't give a tinker's fuck about her juicy fantasies and I just wanted to get it on in the old-fashioned Me Tarzan, You Jane style, dig?

"But I get so many hang-ups that way," she whined . . . I could hear her false eyelashes clicking rapidly from across the room. I refused to believe my sense of hearing.

"I'll be fucked in half!" I screamed. "You're willing to dress me all up in drag, smoke tons of grass, shoot speed, pop poppers and have me play your mother in bed and you are telling me you're uptight about a simple screw?"

But I just resort to throwing her down on the bed and forcing an old fashioned on her. She began to dig it. In fact she began to dig acting like a woman again with a man on top of her so much that, within minutes, we had gone counter clockwise to the other extreme on the sex cycle. Before I knew it we were into a complete sado-macho-masa master-slave scene with her wallowing at my feet in some outrageous rubber skin suit she had hustled into and me barking orders and cracking a twelve foot bullwhip, which I assume came with her outfit, in the air. I got to admit the whole scene turned me on, but later I thought what a drag this is getting to be.

WINTER 66

I was sitting around the BUCKET OF BLOOD tonight waiting around for Willie Appleears to come back with the dope I sent him to cop from Mancole in the poolroom. I'm sipping a Coke, half on the nod, when in comes some dude right at me raging. He was huge. I braced myself in case this cat was going to rap me. Before I had time to do that, however, he knocked me flying right off the stool and onto my ass, then he kicked my thigh one solid shot and stepped back and stared me over. "Do I know you?" I asked. "You bet your fucking sore ass you know me, prick, you're the weasel that beat me with this hype acid last weekend, give me ten dollars right now or get outside." I told him I was totally broke. "Then get yourself outside," he screams in total madness. "Now look," I tell him, "if we step outside one of us is going to get hurt." I was beginning to get a little pissed off myself by now. "Get outside," he says. I storm off the floor and whiz out the door, he follows. I turn and am greeted by the hardest fiver my jaw ever received. "This guy is pretty tough," I mumble to myself. Then I throw one futile punch and he proceeds to whip me down to the pavement, kick my same thigh, stomp my face and rub my head into the concrete surface. He steps back seeing I had gotten enough, and he was fucking right because I was sore as a goat and had the first bloody nose of my life. I saw Appleears standing there with the dope so that was a major consolation. I got up to hit the woods and get off as soon as possible. I looked right at the big motherfucker and said, "See, I told you one of us was going to get hurt." I may get my ass beat occasionally, but I always get the last word. We tipped to get high in some nice green spot somewhere.

WINTER 66

I told the old lady I been making it with lately that I was packing her in. What brought the whole thing on me was calling her up while I was downtown in her area last night. She was surprised because I usually only see her on weekends ("I guess you got to keep on cracking those school books on the weekdays," she's always saying). I told her I had been running around all day sick and needed money to score. She's always good for plenty of junk money but I used up the weekday allowance she lays on me a little early this week. She said sure and I went up with Brian to get the bread. I was so wiped out by the time I rang her bell (in a bad cold sweat with the shivers rushing up from my crotch out the top of my brain, which felt like it was dismantled from place and would bang against the walls of my head each step) that I agreed to crash there while Brian went to pick up in the village. She handed him sixty dollars and he split. The second the door closed the bitch was all over me. I told her she had no idea how I felt and to just let me lie down and sweat out the wait. Her slightest touch set little stinging grenades off in my head. She did manage to get off my pants and onto the bed we went with the agreement we would just lay still and watch the tube. But she didn't seem able to comprehend my condition and continued to paw me. I was rapidly pissed off but too sick to do anything about it. Suddenly my whole body quaked, I looked down and there she was with her mouth sucking away. It was horrible . . . I rattled with blasts of chills. It felt like someone had put a half dead fish on my cock. I jumped up and slammed her across the face, whipped on my pants over the cramped legs and made for the door.

"What about my sixty dollars, you prick!" she screamed.

"What about my innocence," I said, going down.

WINTER 66

Genie Walsh is doing two years on the Rockefeller program for dealing. This means he's in the junkie prison, that's all the program is about, just a cell and all that bullshit, no medication or nothing. His wife asks me to get her five bags once a week and I always do it for her though she don't do stuff herself and normally I never cop for anyone who ain't got a habit. This is strictly on moral grounds. But I'm hip to her gig; like what she does is empty the five bags into one for visiting hours with Genie upstate and she kisses the bag into his mouth when she leaves him. Then he gotta stick the bag up his ass 'cause they comb you naked before you get back in your cell, they check the mouth first. It's a quick trick, and if you fuck up you screw your wife as well. The only problem then is getting a set of works and man, that's a real bitch to smuggle in no matter how big an asshole you got. So it usually winds up maybe one cat in your cell block got a set stashed and to use them you got to give more than half your dope to him, but now Genie got a set off some dude that got out so he's in good shape. I think if I wasn't on junk every minute if I had two years of my life in the joint in front of me I'd hang myself within two weeks. That scene would leave me loopy.

WINTER 66

Nobody straight with scag down at the poolroom by two p.m. and the same up at Izzy's in the Heights. No panic, no sweat, we had our wake-up shots and all and the streets are ripe with some fairly good powder lately but it's just one of those times no one's around. So Mancole and I hit the park and notice fat dyke Lucy hanging off a bench on the nod smoking and burning a hole in the rag she calls a shirt right over her nipple. We ask who's holding. Turns out she was holding but she just sold out but this guy next to her, just off the boat from P.R. got some zonko brown stuff via Mexico. Jimmy and I huddle. "Brown can be dynamite, remember that last brown we had?" runs down Jimmy. I'm suspicious. "I recall, but Lucy is a queen rip-off artist and who's to take a chance on this twitch via Mex. who most likely never been south of the Washington Bridge bus terminal with his brown dope yes very exotic yesyes but sounds like a lot of sheep shit maybe, huh? you dig?" We stare at each other ten seconds and what the fuck, decide to cop it anyway. End of huddle. If we weren't half stoned we wouldn't have bit like saps but . . . OK, four nickel sacks por favor. I off the $20 to him and we taxi down to headquarters to fix. Jimmy's already ripping a bag in his so meticulous manner into the cooker when I mutter on a whim, "Taste it." He looks up glazed like I'm not all there (you see one dangerous convenience of using junk over a period of years is that you eventually lose any paranoia over the possibility of getting bad dope, like you don't go through all that bullcrap of taste on tongue or "better not shoot it all at once" etc. crap like when you were first starting. After a while you become such a drooling fiend it's just dump it all in, cook, main, and bingo! And if an abscess pops up like an oozing golf ball or if you o.d. or if it turns out it was "Drano" you were banging into your arm, just send the flowers of your own choice . . . blue to match the skin color). So you can imagine Mancole's expression when I called my hunch. But a hunch is a hunch so, slightly pissed, he wets his finger and dips in raising a small taste to his mouth hoping for that familiar bitterness. On the spot he leaps up and tosses the cooker and all on the floor in disgust, sobbing and so hot you can see a dead spic in each eye. I take a taste myself from the spilt pile on the floor and get a strange flash of nostalgia . . . I'm out sick with the 'flu in grade school . . . moms brings me lunch in bed: soup and a glass of FUCKING *Ovaltine!!!* And sure as little poppies bloom, that's what we copped, four bags of the stuff. I ask Mancole if he remembers the stuff too. "We drank *Nestle's,*" he sobs.

WINTER 66

Willie Bender, the king of the drunks in this neighborhood, kicked off today. They found him dead on a park bench right across the street from the Bucket of Blood, the only bar in the whole of Manhattan that would still give him credit. It was a sad end of an era in a way. Willie was famous for going on the wagon for one month or so and then freaking onto a four or five month binge that would mean almost two quarts of straight whiskey a day. He drank like a fish. Lots of taste too. "No wino me," he'd say, "give me a Johnny Walker Red or go fuck yourself." He was a friendly son of a bitch, never a bad head loaded or not. He'd think nothing of going drinking on the park benches with us when we were still too young to drink in the bars and he could rap right along without sounding like a shithead boring drunk. He lived in the park, as a matter of fact, in one of the prettiest sections, where he would refer to a tidy green enclosure as his living room and a bench right beside it as his bedroom. If anybody was ever caught on that bench, he would attack them right off it, then sit around and weep that people had no respect invading a person's bedroom like that. He knew the Cloisters inside out, and he had theories on the reflections of varying social and political conditions as an influence on French sculpture from one century to another. These theories, I hate to say, were completely wrong, as I pointed out to him one day, and he wouldn't speak to me for a week. Everybody at Headquarters chipped in tonight to get him a wreath, though it's doubtful anyone will be able to get up the bread for a wake for the poor guy, and he'll probably be buried over at the Potter's Field, with all the other soulful bums of the Metropolitan night.

WINTER 66

I don't know what the fuck these cats on 16th St. are cutting their dope with, but I can't get off a single shot now without puking. Marty got the same shit, two minutes after the needle's out it's into the john and upsy daisy. Willie can't understand it, neither can Desmond or Kooky . . . it don't bother them in the least. But who the hell cares? These drag queens that are selling there are always home, always carrying, and sell only $10 bags that are excellent in both quality and quantity, empty one of these bags out and you got a happy little white mountain in front of you, so much more convenient than scraping out all these $2 skimpies which require twelve bags for a good hit. If I could rate house connections in Manhattan like Craig Claiborne does restaurants, these questions on 16th and Seventh rate four stars. Only objection is the puking bit, but dig . . . it's no hassle puking while you're getting your rush off this shit. It's fun now. I puke four times a day and I love it now. Puking's the newest thing on the junk scene. Soon *Life* is gonna have a cover story on puking as the new rage, soon the college dudes will have a new campus craze.

WINTER 66

I woke up screaming early this morning. It was a dream, not a nightmare, a beautiful dream I could never imagine in a thousand nods. I was swimming in a giant pool, underwater all through time, though it didn't matter. I think the century was wrong, everyone was dressed old fashioned. And I saw this girl next to me who wasn't beautiful really until she smiled. And I felt the smile come at me and heat waves following, soaking through my body and out my fingertips in shafts of color. And her face is still with me, this strange European face with horribly sad sunken eyes that were like some proof she had never smiled before, until then, and I held her for a minute and she cried and left. And these parents were waiting for her and she was slightly lame, I could see, and they all shoved quick into this old car and drove off. Then I was on the back of the car yelling where was she going and they were taking her to this "home," they kept saying the "home." I saw her look back while they kept saying that word and then I woke. And all day I knew there was an incredible love somewhere in my world . . . and I felt sad, needing to explain it but I can't because it belonged to me, to anyone else it was just wet images. And I got this incredible warm beautiful pain in my veins now trying to sort it all out. It's a long time gone that I have dreamt these dreams in Winter.

WINTER 66

I heard from this guy I played ball with years ago in the Biddy League back down on E. 29th that my old friend Herbie was in stir on a murder rap. Seems he pushed some guy off a roof when he caught the dude trying to run off with money he sent him to cop a quantity of dope with.

"He was dealing pretty big there for awhile," the guy told me nonchalantly, "now he's fucked good."

I asked him what became of the rest of the old Boys' Club bunch. He just mumbled that most of them were either strung out or doing a bit at Riker's Juvenile.

"What became of Bobo?" I asked . . . I remembered the time Bobo spit on me from the balcony above the gym floor and as soon as I got him off guard I broke an unopened bottle of Pepsi over his face.

"Bobo is dead," he lifted his head up, "overdose from two bottles of methadone."

"I never liked the prick anyway," I half laughed, "he spit on me once."

"And then you broke his jaw with a bottle," the guy said, staring weird.

"Right . . . you remember that, huh?"

"Bobo was my brother," he said.

_____ WINTER 66

I am now in Riker's Island Juvenile Reformatory doing three months for possession of three bags of heroin and a syringe. The time before this when I got busted the judge suspended the rap and told me if I came before him again it was time. The judge was not bullshitting when he said that. I'm not interested in keeping this diary going while I'm here. Maybe later. Right now I'm not interested in anything.

_____ WINTER 66

Still at Riker's. I'm still not interested in the diary for now but there is something that flashed in a brain spasm that is buzzing. I was wondering all day, huddled in a broom closet I frequent for hours each day, about what a nice concept it is having a "godmother" and "god-

father" . . . and who my godparents could be. There's
no special reason I thought about, but I'm interested in
getting out of here so I can ask my mother who my
godparents are. My mother refuses to visit me here, so
I'll have to wait.

SPRING
&
SUMMER
1966

SPRING 1966

Though I've only done a month's time, thanks to the plea of my school's headmaster I walked out the gates of Riker's Island yesterday, a "free man," feeling like a cartoon about to run off its reel. So this morning I woke up in a place where, for the first time in thirty-one days I could walk out into the pleasures of concrete and sun at my own will, could sit in Pete the Greek's and order whatever breakfast I want. Order meat that for once did not taste like something from the most remote inner guts of a very sick animal. Last night Headquarters was a castle . . . a filthy castle, so many roaches climbing the walls that if they all opened their mouths in unison I believe it would sound like the barking of Irish wolfhounds. Mancole did me the honor of preparing me a syringe filled with "the finest junk in upper Manhattan." I almost refused . . . it was a moment I had both dreamt of passionately and cursed even more . . . but with the dream in front of me again I found that it was quite easy to curse . . . but so much harder to refuse. It was fine, and I was stoned in nods of black pools with strange insects buzzing. I climbed out the bedroom window and sat on the fire escape for hours . . . I did that for the simple reason that the window had no bars.

So I'm putting this past month behind me for now and for later, and we won't have any more about it. Suffice to say I am finished with the asshole bandits of shower room rape; suffice to say that those swine for guards won't draw blood from my ankles again; suffice to say nobody will hang himself one night on the other side of a wall six inches thick from where I sleep; suffice to say I won't have to watch anymore fourteen-year-old

Puerto Ricans carving their initials in forearms with filthy dull forks they stashed, taken off to the infirmary a week later for blossoming gangrene; suffice to say no black cell-block kings will stab fat little Jews here . . . suffice to say that I found a broom closet at the end of my cell-block where I could hide from the ugly screws and filthy cock and sad-eyed forms and learn to love silence and suffice to say that, though I spent four hours a day in that closet, I didn't become pure on Riker's Island.

SPRING 66

I saw Diane Moody breezing along 200th St. today with her distinct whore bop. I crossed the street to hit her for a bean to cop. She just got back from some guy's place in the sticks upstate where she was kicking a pretty heavy habit cold, "with an occasional downer now and then," as she put it. She looked foxy as ever with a tight white mini and her vogue shades and actually more to-gether-looking than I ever saw her since she started on dope a couple of years back. I told her this and she smiled. She was the type that started with a shot now and then out of the romantic notion that dope has some fatalistic charm that stacks chicks like her over straight chicks. That is to say she got tired of screwing everyone in the neighborhood and wanted something to justify her stopping it without seeming like a drag. She got strung out about six months after this notion hit her, and wound up fucking old men instead to keep up her head. We were always pretty tight so she gave me the dollar and I told her how great it was that she wasn't using anymore. I said I'd see her around and she walked on. I imagine she'll be strung out again within two weeks or so.

SPRING 66

End of L.S.D. era last night . . . very bad scene, like getting gulped up in a dream. Gulped by the big city. Ate my blue tab in the "A" train but, on arrival, none of the Friday night prep school acid eaters' club to be seen in the park. "Fuck 'em," say I, "I'll go solo," and I popped another tab. And I went so, so low. Reach the Museum of Modern Art and I began to feel my oats. Those flowers they leap right off that canvas at me. Those flowers, they choke. And it is right then that I realize something is happening that has never happened before: I AM ALONE . . . and not just me doctor, WE'RE alone. Alone forever and who's at the end of that forever tunnel I run through up Fifth with wallpaper of sky-scrapers? And I'm thinking, after all those beautiful trips, that this is one of those *bad* ones . . . and, shit, they are bad indeed. Alone. Go to Bellevue . . . get down . . . but I just vision bearded doctors with patches sewn on their foreheads, "Don't call us, we'll call you . . . eventually," and all those white rooms, TOO WHITE. Alone is white.

So I run to 72nd and call Steve, "I is on the bum, you please come?" He raps, "Give me five minutes." I wait and wait but five minutes is a long time when I can watch the seconds go by like each car that passes. So I split across town: W. 72nd, alone on the second worst street in New York. Horrible cartoon people bop past me. And then meet Blonde Sheila and her hospital voice . . . she takes me in her pad, feeds me pills and blanks the gulp on my trail. So today I say pass the spike, *por favor*. And better to be strung out a thousand years than another night like that. Now we see what the white powder brings.

SPRING 66

I spent a good fucking sick morning trying to cop dope today but not a soul in the neighborhood is holding. "Just got my wakeup shot for the morning and this evening," is all I hear. "Heard there's been a big bust on 134th and nothing's happening at all." And that's the line I hear from every dealer I see, which wasn't too many 'cause sixteen saps got busted last night either in the pool room or in front of the candy store or in the projects, narcs just breezing right on into every other pair of pockets they could find. Steaming hot around here, like someone got busted and is feeding out names to save his own ass like a homing pigeon in heat. So for me it's back to the subway and down to the Village where on E. 2nd Street I spot amigo Kookie and his chick Diamond. They had the same story but did have methadone to sell, insisting it was good. I'm good friends with both, we been through a lot of N.Y. scenery together hunting a bag in winter midnights. I trust them as much as you can a junkie which ain't much no matter who it is but no time to be picky anyway. I've had methadone before and I have a very high natural tolerance to it but two hundred milligrams can do the trick so I give them eleven bucks, a good deal for that amount, and down the bottle, right on the spot. That's the shit with methadone, it's cut with Tang or O.J. so dealers can easily cut the shit, but this stuff was bitter enough so I figured it was OK. Of course the other hassle is you can't shoot the stuff and it takes a good hour at least to hit before you feel them warm oats settling down your sick belly. You bet that's a long hour too, with them cold flashes shooting up from your crotch right out your skull and your muscles feeling like wood and your energy to a sad eyed drip. Yep, I'm good and sick without that fix now and my rap of being the one who can keep it all under control is in that breeze cluttered with the same raps a million times run down by a million other genius wise ass cats walking like each other's ghosts around these same sick streets in my same sick shoes. So then the methadone is pumping that warmth back in me by now and I'm together again, but I ain't high worth one short nod, the high is all in the past . . . I'm just another normal body now functioning like all the other faces I pass going back uptown though they ain't laying out bread to get that way. But fuck all that 'cause once Mr. Jones got you by the back even self pity ain't worth shit, though it's about all most junk heads got left. More money equals less head. And that's the way it is and you know and you know.

SPRING 66

I'll admit it, I have to, that today I had an experience hustling fags that, for once, turned me on. Quite a bit in fact. There's this porno movie house on 14th Street and, though the films are strictly girlie, there's a large clique of fags who hang around the men's room and the tiny lounge outside it down in the basement. Hungry variety of all sorts of gays ready to stalk like sissy falcons. The scene works like any subway "peek on the sneak" gig; you're taking a piss and a quick shuffle breaks out for the adjoining urinal and the fruit starts whacking his doodle, eyes zeroed in on thy neighbor. I work mine up hard, stick out my hand flashing three fingers, he takes out thirty bills slow and somber (I can see this place ain't used to hustles, the dude probably figured he was copping a freebie) and shoves it into my pocket, climbs down the fingers to his blood-throbbing purchase and gives a few nimble yanks on it. By now I've realized that the door at the top of the stairs is intentionally loud so that everyone gets back to normal, so to speak, positions until a lookout near the door gives the OK all clear that it's not the boys in blue: so corny ass a procedure that it's a bit sexy in some melodramatic sense. Anyway, a few more giggles with the wrist and my man is on his knees as everyone scrambles in from the lounge outside and circles around ringside while he begins humming a familiar tune down below.

Now I must tear from my soul's depths, out of faithfulness to the muse of truth, and admit the strange pleasure cast on me by this naughty act of perversion for profit . . .

But, bullshit aside, some weird sensation *did* shoot a blood rocket up my zone as an incredible rush of power shook me with all those faces staring at my body fucking a mouth on its knees . . .

Hordes of different faces, I scan each. Some so nasty, some total femmes in drag, S&M freaks with their hard butch crewcut stares (those leather freaks look tough but they can't fool me because once you get them alone in bed they pay and they lay on their belly to be fucked as dainty as any queen), then there's the inevitable old grey genial chaps, no other sex for them anymore but to look on and remember . . . I've seen them all & I see them now, slobbering fat heroes . . . some jacking off right open, others just clutching it inside, sometimes swapping feels off each other. I begin to fantasize on each as I start getting hotter and hotter: I see all the teachers I've ever had, fat principals, basketball coaches, an old superintendent from 6th Street age seven, famous poets from all times down . . . a giggling drag queen unshaven in the corner, he's all the girls I've ever fucked; I see cops who busted me, judges, oh yes, *all* the judges, drooling . . . the door slams upstairs and a sudden pause, an uptight Jew signals the OK, he looks at me with soft assurance in his voice . . . says, "It's all fine, go ahead," as he became the one man from my past I hadn't seen, watching now too as I shoot hard into the mouth beneath and hurry to zipper up, watching the faces change back to black and white cartoon old men, obscure members of the cosmopolitan night.

SPRING 66

People are always branding junkies the slob wastes of society. Not so, chumps. The real junkie should be raised up for saying fuck you to all this shit city jive, for going on with all the risks and hassles and con, willing to face the rap. Know this: there's different type users of junk.

You have your rich dilettante square ass who dabbles now and then, always has the bread handy to take off to the Riviera if he feels he's fucking around to any danger point, and always with some sap to cop for him so he never gets busted when there's heat. Street junkies hate these pricks but they're all suckers and their money makes them tolerable. Most of them are the jet set, east side bar types they been writing about in *Life* magazine lately, sports cars and all, a lot of rock and roll dipshits who want a head now and then. Then there's the upper middle class Westchester weekend dope heads, preppies and them, same type as the other basically. Come to Harlem to cop on Friday or bring some up to the campus after Christmas. They always get the worst dope or get beat for everything, now and then with a knife in the back. What they been good for lately is opening up their daddies' and mommies' eyes to this horrible "social virus" so that the government gets static from the power people for the first time. So now all these rehabilitation programs are being hustled up and junkies are finally getting treated like humans on the street and in the joint. If the shit remained in the ghetto, black or white, like it had for years nobody would give a shit what happened now or later. Then there's us street kids that start fucking around very young, thirteen or so, and think we can control ourselves and not get strung out. It rarely works. I'm proof. So after two or three years of control, I wind up in the last scene: strung out and nothing to do but spend all day chasing dope. Any way counts, folks. No way to any Riviera and no rich momma to run to. Like you just know when you're in the real junkie thing when you wake up in the morning and say to yourself and know it and go through with it, "Today I either get my fix or get my ass busted into the Tombs, fuck it all."

SPRING 66

Bad times lately, big panic on dope in the streets and as a result prices zing ever upward. Under dialectic (I learned that in school) rules of junk, the means of getting up bread to score must become more profitable than hand-bag snatching and knife-to-neck park profits. So tonight fat Henry, me, and some eager redneck ass-kissing neo-phyte we could all do without go down to some dumpy new bar and disco go-go dive off 96th and Second to hear this old friend of mine and his band play at the gala opening (fizzzz). The bar is strictly sleazo Astoria bar hounds, worms for go-go dancers . . . Fat Henry got bigger tits, and the band is strictly from "Louie Louie," side B. I tell my friend play Dylan . . . "Who he?" Bring down direct, we duck out. Time to begin our new money-making industry: stealing cars.

Now I have no connections in the hot car line but I'm a master at lock slapping and hot wiring, the two essentials needed to steal one, so I figure steal now, connections later. A "slapjack" is a gizmo about as big as a very long screwdriver, with a weight on it that slides down after you insert the pin at the bottom into the lock on the car door. Bang! you slap down the weight toward the pin and it demolishes the fucking tumblers in the lock. Open door. Then to "hot wire" the heap, in this case a new Porsche (what else?). That's just a matter of connecting the right wires under the dashboard and put, put, putttt. So our asshole pal hops into the driver's seat with a claim to fame glare all over his mug and the three of us pull out. From here on all that seemed to remain was to hop on the East River Drive right on 96th, get uptown and stash it on one of those god-forsaken streets around the auto graveyards up near the neighborhood. I had this friend I did a short bit with in the juvenile house on Riker's Island who I knew would have some cat ready for this type of thing, and then there was always old Herbie from the Lower East's big brother who taught us all how to "hot wire" cars age twelve, the diaper bandits, and I'm sure he could set up a deal. Meanwhile asshole is flying and weaving up the Drive like a maniac and we got to cool him down every ten seconds from getting yanked over by the man and blowing everything. (I think I laid down that last attempt at car stealing I was involved in in a previous diary, no? When we got chased, ran up a pole and got busted?) But luck hangs with us this time and despite the mad cowboy at the wheel we run off the Drive at Dyckman St. and spin over to Headquarters. I map out a safe dark side street near the dump to the asshole where he can store the car while Fats and I pop up to HQ and get on the phone to try and score a deal. There were only three guys upstairs when we came in, Brian and Moocher were stoned on the sofa watching a movie with a hookah sitting between them. Mancole was in his nod chair-bed zonked in foetus pose. I figured Herbie's brother, Ron, was the best bet after all, so I got him on the phone and he told me he had a guy in the East Bronx who handles hot Porsches like cashews. He says we can probably make the deal tonight and that he'll get in touch with the cat, call us back, and probably drive up and meet us . . . I tell him I can cut him in even and he says we should haul in about three hundred each. That probably means more like two and a half but I know nothing about the going price for this sort of thing so I'll settle for anything around that area. While we're waiting for him to call back I snuck into Mancole's stash and swiped a paper of dope, I had just come out of the bathroom after banging up when our shithead third partner walked in with a few other people he found down the bar. He was rapping out the whole night's scene to them in fluent bullshit and proceeded to tell the tale to everyone who came in thereafter, sewing on a frill of crap each time he spiced out the gig. I was wondering what was taking Ron so long (it was two hours now and he hadn't called) when he turns up at the door with some fat little Italian guy. Moocher, stoned, ran up to the wop and handed him a couple of bucks . . . The dumb fuck thought he was the man delivering the pizza he ordered.

From here we drive over to where asshole had parked the thing and also from here this diary becomes very anti-climactic and, in fact, quite a fucking bringdown for all concerned. It seems asshole didn't read a few signs that happened to be sprinkled everywhere you looked: TOW AWAY ZONE . . . NO PARKING AFTER SIX P.M. Oh my god did I sink when I saw a yellow light spinning on top of a tow-truck and the familiar cherry red of the man-mobile lighting up the weedy piece of pavement surrounding our Porsche. Henry and I turned to the asshole with an honest, articulate gesture. The Italian fellow, not a very astute observer it seemed, says, "Uh, where youse got it, in a garage or somethin?" "Just keep on driving," I tell him. So long, car copping business.

SPRING 66

Got up early this Saturday morning for a change, got to meet Al Dolan who is going to come with me down to the American Legion Post on 207th St. so we can hustle some bread. We got there and Al keeps the boss man busy while I swipe a dozen raffle books so we can sell them around here for $2 a book. It wasn't any hassle slipping away the books off the table and into the cut-away inner lining of my coat while Al rapped some shit to the guy about how rude the raffle sellers that came to his building were and that he was here to issue a complaint. The old fish offered his sweet apologies to Al and out we went, $24 worth of raffles in my trusty inner lining.

We started selling around Sherman Avenue and got rid of four books on that street alone. The donkey Irish around here would buy anything in the name of God's Holy Legion so this, you see, is easy bread for crooks like us on any given gloomy Saturday, too wet for ball games in the park and too broke from drugs or drinks.

Our luck began to dwindle a bit as we hit the Jewish section of the neighborhood up the hill in ritzy Overlook Terrace, but, still, within an hour or two we were both down to one book each and anxious to get rid of them so we could go get high somewhere. So we're working this building back down on 204th St. and I get rid of my last book and turn to Al with appealing eyes, but he has one book left to go. He raps on a door and out comes this piece of twat older woman in a tiny little frilly nightgown, oh my lord, what a pair of tits has she! "Can I do something for you boys?" she asks. I could have choked on the spot. I chime in (since Al has gone into

semi-petrification), "Well, my friend here and I are selling these raffles and you can win a brand new Mustang
in the drawing next week if you take a chance with one
book, price $2." "I'm afraid I'm out of cash right now,"
she said, "but would your friend and you like to come
in for a drink anyway; you *do* drink, don't you?" Yes
indeed we do. Yes, and we go right in and sit right over
on the couch as we wait for her to come back with two
tall screwdrivers, sitting right between the two of us. Call
me Oedipus if you will, but I was piping, older ladies
really turn me on and by now we knew she was for real
and not some crazy old lady in Grand Central Station
or something that gets the thrill out of leading you into
some abandoned part of the station and then yelling for
the National Guard when you come near her. So halfway
through the drinks she reaches her hand down our pants
and twiddles away on our things, tuga-tug tuga. "Nice
tall young men, ain't you?" What a bonus this is, and
what a hard-on I've got . . . tuga-tuga-tug. Zippers
down . . . tug . . . I won't describe too much . . . tugatug
tuga, except that she was a handjob freak and she just
kept tugging away as we went to play on her body. There's
nothing like unexpected sex, especially when selling raffles for the American Legion, so we both came in a
matter of minutes, she licking her fingers off and zip-
pering back up our pants just like in the dirty books I
used to hide under my rug a few years before. Actually
I think they're still there. But that was that, and out the
door we went, invited back anytime. Nice lady, and you
would be surprised by the number of women like her.
Some just like to tease you by answering the door in
skimpy outfits and all, but others actually invite you in
and follow up. Any salesman knows this is true, not just

a story in the movies, and you can bet I got her apartment number in my head right now. But Al still has one book to go and here he is still trying to get rid of it. Finally he loses control and when some old lady don't answer the door, he starts yelling like crazy Otto or something and saying how she hates the church and how doomed she is in the name of the Lord and pounding away all along. Then she opens up the peekhole on her door and tells Al that he better be cool or else she's gonna call the man on him. Al goes right up to the peekhole instead and starts making incredible faces at the old bugger and, dig this, she pokes a giant pencil right into Al's mug, drawing blood from all over the lip. I had to laugh my nuts apart at the genius of this lady, but Al seemed to fail to get the joke and after spitting a giant goober all over the old bag's door, he ran out of the house and into the street, raging like some insane monk. With Al's lip pouring with blood, we decided to fuck the last book and pool our earnings for a spoon of cocaine. And that's exactly what we did and for the rest of the day we ran around rapping with that great cocaine buzz and tinge and feeling just fine.

_____ SPRING 66

Took peyote buttons today (magic mushroom of Mexican Injuns) with Marc Clutcher who snuck the shit back from Mexico in his tape recorder. He told me he took some down there with the Indians and some other "gringos" and the scene was everyone like, say, nine cats in one big teepee-like tent, in a circle, eating the buttons and sipping tea made with the stuff, sitting silent for ten hours straight, without moving and no leaving . . . just pure cosmic buzz throughout, no music or lights or any bullshit they've been pawning off since *Life* discovered L.S.D. and the media went ape and the narcs made it illegal. Shit, it was so nice when we first got it two years back when nobody knew about it and we got pure stuff and not the home made shit they're pawning off now loaded with methadrine and who knows what.

I ate a bunch of them, so did Marc, and after twenty minutes we got that nauseous feeling really bad but hung on so we didn't puke it before it got in the system. After an hour, Marc puked, but he was feeling it come on so it was OK. I strangely felt a bit better and didn't have to. The experience was incredible, it was different than acid and I didn't figure on that. As usual I can't describe the thing in words, I'd just waste time. One thing did happen that never happened on acid: I got one complete, total hallucination. It was in Central Park near the lake and I watched a weeping willow turn into a giant rooster and fly off. No tree remained. It glided beautifully into the sky, a big blue barnyard. My mind went with it, somewhere all you bald headed generals and wheelchair senators could never imagine.

SUMMER 66

I'm sitting on the john seat in Headquarters, been up sick for three days trying to kick cold, but the habit has really caught up with me this time and got me licked real nasty. So now's as good a time to lay down just how it feels, though the idea of writing seems like so much bullshit now anyway . . . but no way to turn over and forget it . . . to sleep like that cock-sucking janitor must be sleeping downstairs because the place is freezing and the radiator next to me is cold running like a sick nose.

So I'm bundled here with my coat still on and two blankets too and just when the warmth takes over your body it spreads into horrible flashes of heat flushing on through until you peel off the blankets and the rushes of cold shoot up from your balls right on out the skull. And then the cramps in the guts and the horrible shitting, in fact I think today is going to be the worst of all . . . and you just never know what's coming next because no two junkies get the same sickness. I never puke, but Mancole and fat Henry can't stop when they got it. My worst part has to be the horrible fits of sneezing that come over me, sometimes they last five minutes straight . . . and when I walk the inside of my head begins to shake like it's all fallen apart and the way the blood just stops its flow which takes you back to that clammy cold death freeze, toe to head and the hot and cold ripples, the shit etc . . . and to think I have to kick this now because I got to get back to fucking HIGH SCHOOL in two weeks! What a fucking joke, I mean I just can't believe how unslick I feel.

SUMMER 66

It's been about a week now since I put down any entries in this diary, in fact the last one I wrote must have been a bit off key since I had been cold turk three days when

I scribbled it down on that fucking cold toilet seat in H.Q. To tell the truth my "withdrawal" only lasted one more day before I shot up a bag of smokin' stuff I snuck out of Mancole's coat pocket. Now I'm back as good or bad as ever, hustling around . . . three of us just took off some dog walker up in the park today for his watch and wallet, which means I'm back to the old knife and gun holding scene too. I don't dig that shit really but I'm so disgusted with hustling queers that it's my only way out now.

What did set me thinking was this therapy rap session I went to last night with a few other H pals. Some lady professor there asked at one point if we weren't scared of the drug scene, then weren't we at least feeling guilty about using junk. I think now and that pisses me off. Like just what is guilty or who is guilty for fuck sake? Big business dudes make billions come out of their ass and they ain't shelling out a reefer's worth of tax. Kids walk through some jungle I don't know how far away and shoot people, and white haired old men in smoking jacket armchairs make laws to keep it all going smoothly. I swim in the river and have to duck huge amounts of shit and grease and "newly discovered miracle fibers" every five feet I move because those smokestack companies don't give a flying fuck . . . Shit my man, it's so *all there* that no one's seeing it anymore. And it's dumb-ass of me to bring it up even now because it's all so much bull-pap corn and I cut out of that a long time ago, so maybe that's why I don't feel too guilty right now . . . come back later, prof.

You just got to see that junk is just another nine to five gig in the end, only the hours are a bit more inclined toward shadows.

As for fear . . . if you wanna play, you got to pay. If
you can't dig that, then haul your ass out quick, or better
still, "Take a hard look down that long corridor," as The
Man said, wiseguy.

—————— SUMMER 66

Getting up around six a.m. these days . . . go fishing for
early morning constitution freaks up in Fort Tyron Park
for sunrise rip-offs. Resorting to sticking knives up to
people's necks for junk money is always an indication
to me that things are pretty bad off. Despite the Madison
Avenue spewings on the subject, junkies do not enjoy
the hassle of this type of fund raising, and are usually
as scared and vulnerable as the victim if any real need
for violence arises. Personally it's the last con I resort
to . . . only when the bread is really tight and there's no
other score around, and even then the cop fear and
general bother of the whole this is usually not worth it.
Yesterday would bear me out on that . . . we were up in
the park for three hours and the only safe shots we could
manage were one lady for five and some other lame for
two and change. Then later in that day it turns out I
get a break and clip a parcel off the back of a truck
outside the drugstore and it turns out to be a gross of
combs. Now on paper that may sound like a score strictly
from Wheaties in your grass but you can really make
out on little items like this. They were good solid rubber
combs (with a little clip on the side like a pen for wearing
in shirt pocket) and they were marked 49¢ right on the
plastic casing on them. I banged up a three buck bag

and reeled around the park and basketball courts selling them for 20¢ each or ten for a buck and wound up getting rid of $22 worth of pocket combs.

But today it's back to more cop jitters and rip-offs. While the dog walkers are strolling with their little dears in front tugging along we're right behind in the bushes dreaming of fat wallets. And today our dream came in. A middle aged male, blatantly fruit in manner and dress (his hair bleach-blond crude and in a pitifully ridiculous way almost as long as mine) was swishing by in, eventually, such an outrageous merriment that it was a direct threat to his civil rights. We had to do all we could not to fall out from the bushes howling. But he was a grade A mark and there was no way we were gonna blow it. Luck came all out for our gig today because we hadn't seen one other soul in the park all morning ... it was drizzling slightly and the cop who patrols the park on that half-ass motor scooter would be stuffing donuts and coffee in some greasy spoon. We made a move. Nothing fancy, just bush to victim ... knife to throat. He went stiff as frozen fruit.

"Just keep very silent and still," I spoke, "my friend has a gun and this knife could cause a bad leak."

Mancole got the wallet, a separate wad, his change ... I slipped off his watch, a real sparkler, and tapped his two rings. He handed them over.

We told him we were going to excuse ourselves now. I put my hand to his hair:

"That's really pretty hair. We like long hair." (He had no way of knowing my hair was even longer than his because I stuff it all under a beret I wear so I won't be recognized, I made out like I was down on long hairs too.)

"We like long hair because it's easy to get a good grip on it when you slit a person's throat if he yells for the cops within the next ten minutes."

(This tough ass rap I would spin off while taking a sap off never ceased to amaze me. Actually, it helps cover up the sound of my two knee caps chattering against each other.)

But now we're back at Headquarters totalling up: Five twenty dollar bills and one ten in the wallet, the wad was very thick but it turned out to be all singles, thirty-one. The watch is a fairly new *Bulova* and could get a nice price for hock . . . one nice jade ring and one with his initials and fake birthstones surrounding it. Today turned out to be worth the fears . . . and for the next few days we're gonna be sleeping late.

SUMMER 66

Was rapping with an old friend and dope hustling companion Franky Pinewater tonight up at Headquarters. He's got a beautiful head and we've spent a lot of nights together on acid on rooftops at night digging the star dome and rapping about the mystic. Thing is that Franky's about five years older than me so when we started using scag a few years back he didn't have school to hold him back from a heavy habit like me, so he did go all out from the beginning. Thus he's been very down and out for quite a while and I'm just feeling the pains of my first habit. I never thought he'd end up strung out, but like we were saying tonight: both peyote and opium grow from the earth, and though all the hip dudes are running around raving about all the knowledge of the cosmos peyote gives, who's to say the poppy has no secrets either . . . and though it was me that spouted that theory I don't think I really believe it.

Anyway Franky was telling me how his mother, a fanatical Irish Catholic like so many of the old ladies around here, was just so sick of all the cures he took that failed that she decided to drag him off to High Mass last Sunday and go through the whole bit. It seems Franky had been getting back into the Faith himself lately, reading a lot of Bible and all, and was all for a play at Mass again. What the hell, he tried every other cure in the book, he might as well take the religious route. Too bad, it all flopped. He said that as soon as he sat down (he hadn't had his morning fix yet so he was craving bad, if any miracle was gonna go down it was gonna have to be a biggie) there he was with a side altar to his right stacked with hundreds of those tiny thick candles in the red glass . . . just like the ones we clipped out of that same church to get a nice solid flame to cook up the dope on windy nights in the park (I got one right in the next room, in fact). So he's there staring at these candles imagining a little spoon or twist-off bottle cap over each with bubbling dope within. Then the altar boy walks toward the altar lugging a giant candle . . . and it's visions of glassine stamp holders the size of shopping bags and a ten foot long soup spoon over that candle cooking pounds of junk from powder to sweet juice. By this time his mother was looking at him funny, he's staring dead ahead in a trance like he's picking up a revelation from God, all this stuff floating around his head . . . DOPE. But the topper came when the priest started shaking the incense burner out to the people and Franky caught a good whiff. "It was the absolute, exact same smell as dope when it's cooking, no mistake about it," he rapped (and this is true, now that I think about it, dope cooking has that same heavy musty smell just like that thick church incense they use at funerals and stuff). "What happened then?" I asked him. "What the hell do you think happened, for Christ sake, I got up, left, and tore ass home to my bottom drawer and emptied my entire stock into the cooker and over the red candle . . . stoned."

SUMMER 66

Who did I run into today but old Ju-Ju Johnson, fattest junkie I know, could hide a complete set of works, a cooker and innumerable bags of dope in the layers of fat that flop one by one down toward his belt like a drenched wedding cake. I've seen him do it. Often. Must be a year since I've seen him last. I remember the day, in fact. I was skinny dipping in the Harbor and Ju-Ju, who must be at least fifty, by the way, was standing around watching. Standing too close as it turned out, because this big scumbag hit Johnny Gator in the nose as he was submerging from a dive. Ju-Ju, who makes no sound when he laughs but just opens his mouth and begins to shake like an epileptic mound of Jello, guffawed himself right off the dock in his brand new pinstripe suit he had to go all the way to a fucking fat man's shop in Elmira, N.Y. to get. We were choking in hysterics at the sight when it was brought to notice that Ju-Ju was not too slowly drowning and fatly gulping for aid. Six of us fished him out and he stormed off, a mass of

embarrassment in shrinking pinstripes. And that was the
last of Ju-Ju till now. We come right on to each other
with all that "what's happening? are you straight? something good?" etc. junkie greetings which for once paid
off because Ju-Ju in fact had something quite, quite good
that he turned us on to up in his new apartment. Nice
joint too. For now, that is, 'cause it won't be long. Old
Fats is gonna be pawning the entire furnishings with his
habit. I was nodding heavy as a wet sheet. Grade "A"
check.

Later we rapped about our old con trick we used to
pull every couple of months for a pile. It's a kinda unique
one, in fact, the way we handled it, Ju-Ju and I hit the
nearest welfare joint. I play his son. We crack right off
to the lady our mess: that my moms has croaked; no
food, no house (sleeping in the park), no vitamins or
milk for his baby, me (I was about thirteen-fourteen at
the time, last two years really). He's got a wound from
the war, I was born with one lung. Old moms died slowly
over six years of cancer spreading. Hospital soaked
Ju-Ju like wet cotton. Ju-Ju did the rap (and he could
go on for four whole WD-00199 forms). He was a champ.
I'd just look in teary-eyed despair holding hands on
lap . . . a whimper now and then when mother's death
popped up. "Not those hard benches again tonight dad,
please dad." Dig. Out we walk with a fat emergency relief
check with extra for me, the dutiful son. We hit every
Welfare Center in Manhattan within five days working
fast. That could come to $4,000 at times. Trick was to
work fast . . . Cash fast. And never come back to "follow
up" after the emergency digit. Of course, four months
later, another name (fake I.D. was Ju-Ju's forte), another
case worker and another batch of emergency checks.

Sweet, sweet set-up and no sweat really 'cause it takes them months to process those emergency checks. A lot of fixes from that game, a lot. Thing is Ju-Ju is still working the circuit. "I've been out to some new joints in Staten Island lately . . . wonderful hearts there, free coffee and donuts while you wait—Some even give me cash there for cab fare back." Yes, this is a hard, cold city, but it shows there are the good souls out there too. *Next day:*

I went over to Ju-Ju's and asked him if he thought I could still pass as his son, that welfare con nostalgia seemed so great last night. "No chance," he lays it down, "that long hair of yours, your features filling in, naw, like you got the junk halo now all over. No more innocence, man. And frankly you look totally seedy." What the fuck, he turned me on again to a nice day of nods at least.

——————————— SUMMER 66

I'm familiar with just about every junk pusher from 190th St. up to 225th St. Jimmy Mancole, out of his junkie necessity, probably knows even more. But today we must have knocked on every door and checked out every street corner among all these possibilities and not one dealer was holding a single bag. This is equal to walking down Fifth Avenue at lunchtime on a weekday afternoon and finding the entire street abandoned. I was a mixture of stoned disappointment and anger because I was planning a pleasant day in nod land, but Mancole was in complete sickness and hugging his last nerves. By the time we had exhausted all possible sources he had considered suicide close to fourteen times and must have stopped on every third corner to puke.

"It's those fucking Russians," he kept muttering, "the big bomb's coming at 3 this afternoon, something's happening man, someone's doing this to me." It was a bit rare, I thought.

So we hopped onto the "A" train and made it down to my old neighborhood on 29th to see if I could muster something up but the one guy I was sure of scoring off, Herbie Hemslie, was in the clink now for six months already for pushing some dude off a roof one night. I used to play ball with him less than three years ago, and now here he is up the river on a murder rap, it made me wonder a bit where I was heading. "Chinatown," Mancole yelled, "that's it, there's always someone on the street down there." Super, I thought, total intrigue, maybe we even get to smoke the old opium in the back of some laundry.

By this time Mancole was reeling in total madness, in the cab down there he kept singing, "Motherfucker, sisterfucker, blue ball bitch," then he'd look at me with this insane smile and whisper, almost sing it in fact, "A bitch is a female dog, a bitch is a female dog . . ." etc.

Then we hit Mott St. and bolt the cab because it was some old man driving and he didn't even bother to chase us. After a few minutes wait, we were out on the street sniffing around for this young chink cat Jimmy dealt with a year or two ago. Out of the blue come three long haired chinks who pull us aside and mutter, "You people looking to cop?" You bet your oriental asses we are, we implied in a quick nod and followed them into some obscure alley. "This must be the backdoor to the opium den," I whisper to Jimmy. "Oh, fuck you with your opium dens what the hell you think this is, a Charlie Chan movie, let's just get some H and head back up town." At this point one of the guys faces us and asks how much we got to spend. I told him I just wanted $10 worth figuring he was doing fivers and I was planning on getting two anyway, Mancole told him he had $75. "Well, we got excellent crackers, skyrockets like you never seen and very cheap cherry bombs." We look at each other in complete astonishment. These motherfuckers are selling *FIREWORKS*.

After we recover from this lame adventure we hit the streets again and hope to find John Tom, or at least the poolroom where he holds a mild reputation as the hustler top-notch south of Grand St. Finally we stumble onto the place, a real dive with only eight tables dimly lit and seedy and once again me sure the back room is flooded with opium hookahs. John Tom wasn't around at the time but the owner, crusty and looking straight out of a codeine medicine bottle, assures us he'll be about any minute now. Jimmy hits the bathroom and coughs up his fifth Italian ice, both his and my diet for the day. I do in a few chumps at nine ball (not a very cool move judging from the ill looks that start closing in) and finally in steps Tom. Hordes of nodding orientals stare up and make it over to him assuring us he's carrying. After he deals out his wrappers to the regulars he spots Mancole and struts over to see what we want. Jimmy hands over his seventy-five beans and pockets twenty-five bags amid various ohs and ahs from the onlookers. I get three, using my nine ball winning for a joy bag. Within five minutes we're back on the subway and heading up to

Headquarters cooking up in an instant and leaning back against the chipped plaster tuning our nods in and out of a crumby George C. Scott drama. I hope for Mancole's sake that the same ordeal ain't gonna pop up tomorrow, but that's a long ways off from where we're at now.

SUMMER 66

In ten minutes it will make four days that I've been nodding on this ratty mattress up here in Headquarters. Haven't eaten except for three carrots and two Nestlé's fruit and nut bars and both my forearms sore as shit with all the little specks of caked blood covering them. My two sets of gimmicks right along side me in the slightly bloody water in the plastic cup on the crusty linoleum, probably used by every case of hepatitis in upper Manhattan by now. Totally zonked, and all the dope scraped or sniffed clean from the tiny cellophane bags. Four days of temporary death gone by, no more bread, with its hundreds of nods and casual theories, soaky nostalgia (I could have got that for free walking along Fifth Avenue at noon), at any rate, a thousand goofs, some still hazy in my noodle. In one nod I dreamt I was in a zoo, inside a fence where, down from a steep stone incline, was a green pond filled with alligators. It seemed at one point I was about to be attacked. About ten 'gators surfaced and headed slowly up the incline, staring directly at me. But just when I seemed pinned against the fence, instead of lunging at me, they just opened their huge jaws in slow motion and yelled, "Popcorn!" At this point a little zoo keeper shuffled out and tossed huge bags of popcorn onto the water. I ducked out through a hole that suddenly appeared in the fence.

Zonked, but I've been slugging away at orange juice all along, anyway, for vitamin C and dry mouth. I just crawl out of the bed at first; don't even attempt my human posture. Think about my conversation with Brian: "Ever notice how a junkie nodding begins to look like a foetus after a while?" "That's what it's all about, man, back to the womb." I get up and lean on a busted chair. Jimmy Dantone comes running in and grabs me, "Those guys that we sold the phony acid to the other day are after our asses if they don't get back the bread." "Go tell them I hate them," I tell him. He splits. A wasted peek into the mirror, I'm all thin as a wafer of concentrated rye. I wish I had some now with a little Cheez-Whiz on it. I can feel the window light hurting my eyes: it's like shooting pickle juice. What does that mean? Nice June day out today, lots of people probably graduating. I can see the Cloisters with its million in medieval art out the bedroom window. I got to go in and puke. I just want to be pure. . .

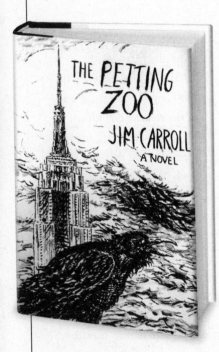

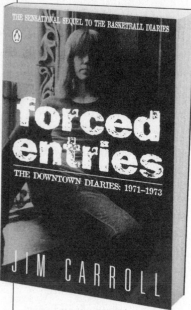